Frank Herbert

Twayne's United States Authors Series

Warren French, Editor

University College of Swansea, Wales

TUSAS 532

FRANK HERBERT
(1920–1986)
Photograph courtesy of Andrew Unangst

Frank Herbert

by William F. Touponce

Indiana University at Indianapolis

Twayne Publishers
A Division of G.K. Hall & Co. • Boston

[redacted]

Frank Herbert
William F. Touponce

Published by Twayne Publishers
A Division of G.K. Hall & Co.
70 Lincoln Street
Boston, Massachusetts 02111

Copyediting supervised by Michael Sims
Book production by Gabrielle B. McDonald
Book design by Barbara Anderson

Typeset in 11 pt. Garamond
by Compset, Inc., of Beverly, Massachusetts

Printed on permanent/durable acid-free paper
and bound in the United States of America

Library of Congress Cataloging in Publication Data

Touponce, William F.
Frank Herbert.

(Twayne's United States authors series ; TUSAS 532)
Bibliography: p.
Includes index.
1. Herbert, Frank—Criticism and interpretation.
2. Science fiction, American—History and criticism.
I. Title. II. Series.
PS3558.E63Z89 1988 813'.54 87-25199
ISBN 0-8057-7514-5 (alk. paper)

To my son Nathan

Some days it's melange; some days it's bitter dirt.

—Rakian Aphorism

Contents

About the Author

William F. Touponce received his B.A. from Hampshire College in Amherst, Massachusetts, and his M.A. and Ph.D. in comparative literature from the University of Massachusetts, Amherst. He is now assistant professor in the English department of Indiana University at Indianapolis, where he teaches children's literature, science fiction, and literary theory. The focus of his work lies in adapting literary theories—traditionally aligned with elite literature—to works of popular culture in order to provide criticism for such works. His first book, *Ray Bradbury and the Poetics of Reverie* (1984), was a phenomenological account of the reader's response to the fantastic, using Continental theorists Iser and Bachelard. Professor Touponce first became interested in Herbert when he discovered *Dune,* which he now includes in his course on science fiction. At present he is preparing a study of Issac Asimov.

Preface

This study of Frank Herbert focuses primarily on the Dune series—*Dune, Dune Messiah, Children of Dune, God Emperor of Dune, Heretics of Dune,* and *Chapterhouse: Dune*—and its compositional structure in an aesthetic sense, which I think is unique among science-fiction series. By all accounts it is one of the most impressive achievements in the history of American science fiction, a genre that has been series prone and filled with multivolume epics since the early days of Edgar Rice Burroughs and his Martian Tales. The science-fiction series has been organized in a variety of ways. It can be loosely knit, as in Robert Heinlein's "Future History" where a number of novels and short stories take place in the same future, but seldom overlap in plot or even characters. It can be almost one continuous narrative, such as Philip José Farmer's Riverworld series in which all of humanity is simultaneously reincarnated on the banks of a ten-million-mile river. Or it can be somewhere in between: Marion Zimmer Bradley's Darkover novels are a collection of episodes in the biography of the planet Darkover.

Unlike other genres, where a series is usually built around a charismatic hero (Sherlock Holmes, for instance), in science fiction it may often be built around an environment, a created world, or a universe. This is certainly the case with the Dune series, for although it presents us with a charismatic hero, Paul Atreides, Herbert is more interested in getting the reader to see the damaging effects these kinds of heroes have on their environments—in short, in ecology. Any reader familiar with the series, or with the reasons for its popularity, knows that ecology is the major theme of the Dune series and its organizing principle just as the "science" of psychohistory is in Isaac Asimov's Foundation series. Although some critics have seen the Dune series as an inversion and parody of Asimov's earlier work, Herbert himself claimed only that the Dune trilogy—*Dune, Dune Messiah,* and *Children of Dune*—was intentionally written as one long ecological novel.

My critical objective in this study is to examine how the notion of ecology evolved in the series as aesthetic strategy and organizing principle. In this regard, it should be mentioned at the outset that Herbert's view of ecology broadened even as he wrote *Dune* to include the study of a whole planetary society—the desert planet he created and called Arrakis. In doing research for the novels, he found fresh nuances of ecology in religion, psychoanalytic theories, linguistics, economics, philosophy, theories of history, geology, anthropology, soil chemistry . . . it's an open list. Obviously I could not present an account of all of these areas of human endeavor that went into the making of the series. What I do provide, however, is an overview of how these various areas, as social discourses, interact in each of the novels as in an ecological system. Excellent specialized studies of the world of Dune—many of them in Willis McNelly's *The Dune Encyclopedia*—have been and undoubtedly will continue to be written. Archetypal readings, psychoanalytic readings, feminist readings—all of these are valid approaches, if only because these discourses are part of the ideological world Herbert created. But in a work as complexly layered as Dune—Herbert called it an "ecological fugue" in which multiple independent voices are heard—parts should not be artificially separated for analysis without being reinterpreted from a sense of the whole, which is in effect a long open-ended dialogue in which many ideologies, as unmerged voices, interrelate. As Liet Kynes, the planetologist of Dune's Imperium remarks, the universe is a place of constant conversation. In reality there are no isolated discourses in the Dune series. Rather, the whole is orchestrated in a "polyphonic" manner so that every voice is qualified, questioned, even subverted, by others. It is this compositional aspect of the Dune series that makes it unique.

My approach to this great conversation is broadly linguistic, treating the Dune series as a kind of social discourse. I have been immensely impressed by certain arguments in Mikhail Bakhtin's *The Dialogic Imagination* (University of Texas Press, 1981), especially by the central claim that the novel can be defined as a diversity of social speech types (sometimes, as in the Dune series, even a diversity of languages, polyglossia and heteroglossia) and a diversity of individual voices, artistically organized by a principle of dialogue. This "dialogized heteroglossia" means that the language of the novel is internally stratified into social dialects, characteristic group behavior, professional jargons, generic languages, languages of generations and age groups, languages of the authorities, and languages that serve specific sociopolitical purposes of the day. It is Bakhtin's view that the function of the novel is to represent or create an image of these languages. Yet the novel does not merely represent. It always includes in itself the process of coming to know another's word, a coming to knowledge whose process is also represented in the novel.

The germ of this study came when it struck me that the ecological layering that Herbert spoke of in discussing the composition of *Dune* (and the mixture of styles some of his critics deplored in the book) was really quite similar to Bakhtin's ideas about the internally stratified language of the novel and its potential for social criticism. Here was a way for me to discuss the book as having some cognitive effect on the reader—as science fiction. But as the study grew, other similarities appeared, especially in the area of the theory of authorship. For Bakhtin, the author himself has to find his own voice among this welter of voices, often by means of a stylistic strategy he calls "double-voiced discourse," in which the author speaks with, or against, his characters who are felt to possess independent voices of their own. Most important in Bakhtin's view is the fact that novels grant authors the freedom to develop, which is to say, freedom to play with their own image on the plane of their own work, which the epic (Asimov's Foundation series) does not.

I have endeavored to show, from a study of Herbert's manuscripts in the archives at California State University, Fullerton, how the Dune series evolved from a basically closed monological design to an open-ended dialogical novel. Chapter 1, which outlines Herbert's biography, depends upon the research of others (unfortunately Herbert died before I had a chance to interview him), but it also attempts to show how Herbert's view of mankind as involved in an ongoing "jam session" with an infinite universe led him to reject all closed systems of thought in his art. In chapter 2 I tell the story of how Herbert arrived, through a crisis of authorship with *Dune,* at the kind of novelistic freedom Bakhtin describes. This chapter also shows how discourses in *Dune*—in this case religion and ecology—interact in the conversations of the characters, and to what extent Herbert revised certain conversations to make them more fully dialogical. In this and in the following chapters I discuss the role of incorporated genres—a one-act play in the banquet scene of *Dune,* tragic poetry in *Dune Messiah,* the journal in *God Emperor of Dune*—as one of the most basic and fundamental forms for incorporating and organizing heteroglossia in the Dune series. Subsequent chapters deal with Herbert's other fiction and with the criticism and reception of his work.

Throughout this study I have been concerned to provide the reader with an overview of the action—something that is not easily achieved since Herbert deliberately frustrates the reader's attempt to construct such a transcendental vantage point from which to view the maelstrom of plots, subplots, and conspiracies that swirl through the thousands of pages that make up the series. Inevitably I have simplified in pointing out Herbert's themes that seem to double back on themselves paradoxically, as in an Escher lithograph. And as for the lengthy enigmatic conversations (often about religion, human evolution, or philosophical ideas like Infinity), even if space permitted, it would be a mistake to pretend to summarize Herbert's immensely varied and aggressively fluid views. For him all "monologue" is faulty, and flat summary is an especially destructive form of monologue. I have opted instead to provide an occasional stylistic analysis that looks closely at double-voiced discourse and how it functions in determining our response, while keeping an eye on the involved counterpoint in the narrative and the overall design of the series as it emerges. Inevitably also in a critical introduction of this sort, which aims to provide the general reader with compact critical analyses of an author's works, I have reduced a multi-accented, complexly orchestrated, polyphonic novel to the range of a piano keyboard. There is probably very little herein to excite a "Dune freak," who in any case probably already knows the major and minor arcana of Dune Tarot. I am confident, however, that a reader new to Herbert's works will, after reading this study, be compelled to turn to the originals, bringing to that reading basic knowledge about the world Herbert created and a fresh critical perspective on it.

I wish to thank Professor Willis McNelly, compiler of *The Dune Encyclopedia* and longtime friend of Herbert's, for reading portions of this study in draft, for providing me with materials in his possession about Herbert, and for making my visit to Fullerton a pleasant one. Any critical judgments or errors expressed in this book are of course entirely my own.

William F. Touponce

Indiana University at Indianapolis

Chronology

1920 Frank Herbert born 8 October in Tacoma, Washington, of Frank and Eileen (neé McCarthy) Herbert.

1938 Graduates high school. At age 19, Herbert moves to Southern California and, lying about his age, gets a job with the *Glendale Star,* thus beginning a career as a journalist on West Coast newspapers that lasts for many years.

1940 Marries Flora Parkinson in San Pedro, California (divorced 1945).

1941 Enlists in the United States Navy and joins the Seabees, but is released six months later on a medical discharge.

1942 Daughter, Penny, born 16 February in San Pedro.

1945 Publishes first fiction under his own name, "The Survival of the Cunning" (a war story set in the Arctic), in *Esquire* magazine.

1946 Attends University of Washington; marries Beverly Ann Stuart on 20 June in Seattle.

1947 Son, Brian Patrick, born 29 June in Seattle.

1951 Son, Bruce Calvin, born 26 June in Santa Rosa, California.

1952 Publishes first science-fiction short story, "Looking for Something," in *Startling Stories.*

1956 Publishes first science-fiction novel, *Under Pressure* (former title: *The Dragon in the Sea*).

1964 "Dune World" serialized in *Analog,* December, 1963, January and February, 1964.

1965 "The Prophet of Dune" serialized in *Analog,* January-May, 1965; *Dune* published, wins the Nebula Award.

1966 *The Green Brain; Destination: Void; The Eyes of Heisenberg. Dune* wins the Hugo Award.

1968 *The Heaven Makers; The Santaroga Barrier.*

1969 *Dune Messiah.*

1970 *Whipping Star.* Begins lectures at the University of Washington on general and interdisciplinary studies.

1971 *The Worlds of Frank Herbert* (short stories).

1972 *The Godmakers; Soul Catcher.* Ends his newspaper career. Retreats to a six-acre farm on Washington's Olympic Peninsula where he divides his time between fiction writing and transforming the acreage into an ecological demonstration project.

1973 *The Book of Frank Herbert* (short stories); *Hellstrom's Hive.*

1976 *Children of Dune.*

1977 *Children of Dune* nominated for Hugo Award for Best Novel. *The Dosadi Experiment.*

1979 *The Jesus Incident* (with Bill Ransom).

1980 *Without Me You're Nothing* (with Max Barnard).

1981 *God Emperor of Dune.*

1982 *The White Plague.*

1983 *The Lazarus Effect* (with Bill Ransom).

1984 *Heretics of Dune.* Herbert's wife of 38 years, Bev, dies of cancer after a ten-year fight against the disease.

1985 *Chapterhouse: Dune.* Marries his former Putnam representative, Teresa Shackleford. *Eye* (short stories).

1986 Dies 11 February at age 65, of a massive pulmonary embolism while recuperating from cancer surgery. *Man of Two Worlds* (with Brian Herbert).

Chapter One

Life and Intellectual Background

Life

To prospective interviewers Frank Herbert usually described himself as a very private man. No private correspondence file has yet come to light in the Herbert archives at California State University, Fullerton, nor is it likely to, since the materials there were carefully selected by Herbert's wife, Beverly. Herbert was not one to bare his soul in his writings, either. Nonetheless, he made no attempt to be unduly secretive about his life, and a basic biography can be gleaned from taped interviews in the archives and from published sources.

What was he like as a person? As a newspaperman, Herbert was very much at ease meeting people. Indeed, he had conducted thousands of interviews in that capacity. That is not to say, however, that he was easygoing. Behind the friendly manner there were walls of privacy and a strong sense of separate identity. He very much believed in traditional American ideas about self-help, independence, and freedom from most kinds of interference. And he did not suffer those whom he considered to be fools. Of his personality, Ben Bova, who was editor of *Analog* in succession to John W. Campbell from 1971 to 1978, and then subsequently executive editor of *Omni,* said: "He was the most *alive* man I've ever met. Frank Herbert was in love with the world, an intensely happy man who was interested in everything and everybody. For much of his life he wore the beard and belly of a latter-day Santa-Claus, but Santa never 'Ho-ho-hoed' as much as Frank did. Laughter came to him as easily as breathing."[1]

In the lectures, readings, and interviews I have listened to Herbert comes across as a man passionately interested in many things—good wine, wind power, ecology, computers, the craft of writing science fiction—and as someone who had personally investigated each of them. On a first hearing his voice seems too highly pitched to fit the image of a portly bearded man, but after one gets used to its peculiar register,

Herbert's voice takes on a rich, resonant intensity that is quite capable of holding an audience enthralled. It is a voice that is sometimes questioning, even querulous, and sometimes almost pontifical in its pronouncements.

But Herbert could also puncture his own inflated pretensions with fits of laughter, or gently mock those who wanted to cast him in the role of ecological guru to the counterculture. He repeatedly warned against the dangers of hero worship as well as ecological abuse. His dominant intellectual impulse was not to mystify or set himself up as a prophet, but the opposite—to turn what powers of analysis he had (and they were considerable) over to his audience. And this impulse is as manifest in *Dune,* which many people consider the all-time best science-fiction novel, as it is in his computer book, *Without Me You're Nothing.* In the latter work Herbert devised, with the help of an expert in the field, Max Barnard, a method to teach readers how to design programs for home computers that would make the computer do a wide variety of tasks, from balancing a checkbook to writing a novel. Thus the title of the book is to be uttered by the programmer facing the computer, and not vice versa.

One salient thing about Herbert that almost everyone who had met him has said is that he loved to talk. He was an ardent conversationalist, delighting in improvisation. Indeed, he referred often to conversation as a "jazz performance."[2] His firmest belief was that the meaning of human life emerges through language, itself a mirror of the ecosystems in which life has evolved. He spoke in general terms about a kind of ecological semantics, pointing out that we commonly believe meaning is found in printed words (such as these), in the noises of a speaker, in the reader's or listener's awareness, or in the thought-land between them. In reality, argued Herbert, meaning arises only out of transactive processes: "We tend to forget that we human animals evolved in an ecosystem that has demanded constant improvisation from us. In a mirror sense, we reflect this history of mutual influences in all our systems and processes."[3] For Herbert, then, dialogue was the principle by which we could tap into an ongoing jam session with our universe, a way to deal with the fact that our survival as a species demands an ever-increasing virtuosity and an ever-improving mastery of our instruments. In his later years he was unhappy with the lecture platform because it was a monologue and allowed him no feedback, no ongoing "jam session," with his audience. He liked to get down off the platform, down on the floor with a radio microphone and talk to individuals, finding out what was bothering them.

Thus it was no accident that his masterwork, the six volumes of the Dune series, is one great orchestrated conversation. Critics who complain about the increasing number, length, and enigmatic quality of conversations in the series are really exposing their own desires for a closed universe, for absolutes that Herbert was unwilling to provide. Indeed, he did not see his own work in *Dune* as a closed ideological system to be contemplated, but rather as something to be actively interpreted, transformed, parodied, exceeded, undermined, and subverted by later volumes in an open-ended dialogue. Closed systems of *all* kinds were anathema to him. As he saw mankind and its environment as part of a total situation, so also he saw in ecological terms that *Dune* was not an aesthetic object to be contemplated, but rather each, reader and text, formed an ever-changing environment for the other during the act of reading. The main character of Herbert's last book, Darwi Odrade, a woman possessed of a vastly powerful analytical mind and equipped with the memories of generations of women before her, finds that she likes the *idea* of jazz. It speaks to her of life, no two performances ever being identical. Players react to what is received from others and so on in a feedback loop. Feed us with jazz, Odrade proclaims, and we will survive as a species (*Chapterhouse: Dune,* 376). This musical metaphor concisely states the training in awareness that Herbert wanted to offer the reader of the Dune series. Ideas in the Dune series will not remain isolated. Our ideas will involve us in surprise encounters with other ideas in an alien environment, in dialogues with others we had not anticipated, where they will be modified and transformed.

Improvisation became something of a principle for Herbert. In the last years of his life he knew the pain of cancer both in himself and in his wife, but "with his own brand of Zen and determination,"[4] he sought ways to get around that pain. Pancreatic cancer is one of the quickest and surest malignant killers. There are no accepted cures. There are very few courses of treatment, even experimental ones, that as much as slow it down. Herbert knew this but nonetheless decided to undergo a new therapy involving heat treatment at the University of Wisconsin. He was, by all accounts, confident of beating the odds. Yet his personal life in Washington and in Maui, Hawaii, with his wife of over thirty years and their three children is likely to remain a private matter (a moving tribute to his wife and an expression of his grief at her loss can be found, however, in an afterword to *Chapterhouse: Dune*). What emerges from his public life and from the recollections of people who knew him well is a man who never lost sight of the fact that life was to be lived, a man with a large appetite for experience who thought that one of the most beautiful things mankind had going for it was surprise. He was convinced that human beings had not finished evolving as a species.

Frank Patrick Herbert, Jr., was born 8 October 1920, in Tacoma, Washington. His father, Frank, Sr., operated a bus line between Tacoma and Aberdeen, later became a member of the newly formed state highway patrol, was chief criminal deputy for Pierce County, in the state of Washington, and later went to Oregon, where he was a safety engineer for the state. His mother was of Irish Catholic ancestry. A sister, still alive today, is his only sibling. Herbert had fond memories of both his parents and grandparents who were among the early settlers in the northwest area of Washington. Frank Herbert, Sr.'s, people came from the hill country between Tennessee and Kentucky in pre-Civil War times. Herbert's paternal grandmother was unlettered, but was known in the family for her remarkable memory of dates, places, and names. It was she who became the "mentat" computer of *Dune*'s Imperium. The many songs she sang while working in the kitchen delighted him as a child. When excited, she spoke in a dialect that resembled Elizabethan English. Herbert traced back his experimentation with dialects and ancient surviving tongues in *Dune* to this early exposure to other languages in his family. His paternal grandfather came to Washington as a civil engineer, but later ran a crossroads country store. Herbert's mother's people emigrated from Ireland during the potato famine to Halifax, Nova Scotia. They traveled under an assumed name as they had been involved in resisting the British and storing up money to buy arms. His maternal grandfather was a Canadian educated as a mining engineer. He also had ten maternal aunts who were the models for the Bene Gesserit matriarchy whose gene-shaping plans span centuries. With a touch of humor, Herbert described himself as a "mongrel" of mixed descent—a lot of Irish, some Semitic, Spanish, and Holland Dutch.

It might be supposed that growing up when he did, Herbert would have had many stark memories of the Depression. Yet he insisted that the opposite was true because his family lived very close to the land in a predominantly rural environment on the Olympic and Kitsak peninsulas:

> A lot of people around the United States look on the Depression as a very traumatic and nasty time. I look on it as one of the most marvelous periods

> of my life. My father didn't have a job. There was one year when I think he made ten or twelve dollars for the entire year. But we lived like kings. We had work. We had a farm and grew all our own meat. We went out and got salmon and smoked them. I took salmon and home grown apples to school with my lunch.[5]

In the same interview Herbert also recalled hunting for deer at the age of eight with his father. When they hunted at night, it was his job to startle the deer with a light so that his father could shoot them. Herbert's father always tried to kill the deer with one shot because bullets cost almost ten cents each—expensive for that time. Even when the family lived on the outskirts of Tacoma they kept chickens and a cow. Herbert also had an uncle who introduced Japanese oyster farming into the Washington area. Herbert learned skin diving and earned much of his money for clothes and schooling by working for this uncle.

Around the age of eight he decided to become a writer, actually announcing his determination on his eighth birthday. His first literary effort was an adventure story about darkest Africa, complete with crayon illustrations. By the time he reached his teens, he was telling stories at Boy Scout campfires: "In a very real sense, I was trained as a *jongleur* was trained, to entertain orally."[6] His education was partly public and partly "classical," at the hands of Jesuits. He remembered always being a bookworm and, during several childhood illnesses, including pneumonia, he read. His first training in writing came in a high school English class. His English teacher, Homer Post, advised the Lincoln High School newspaper and ran his class like a "city desk." Using this experience, while still in his teens, Herbert became a summer replacement for local reporters on the *Tacoma Ledger.* When he was around nineteen, he moved to Southern California and, by lying about his age, got a job with the *Glendale Star.* After the war in 1945, he moved to the *Post-Intelligencer* in Seattle so that he could attend school at the University of Washington; but he was not interested in a degree and stayed only one year to obtain training in fiction writing. He met Beverly Stuart in a short-story class at the University of Washington. They were married in June 1946 and had two sons, Brian, born in 1947, and Bruce, born in 1951 (Herbert's only daughter, Penny, was from an earlier marriage. His first wife, Flora, "Dear Johned" him while he was in the navy). He then worked as a journalist on West Coast papers for many years, holding various positions in the Hearst publishing empire. In 1959 he settled at the *San Francisco Examiner* for over a decade as writer and editor for the newspaper's *California Living* section. Beverly supported Herbert's drive to be a science-fiction writer. He periodically took time off from newspaper work, cared for the children and the house, and devoted himself to writing while Beverly continued to work as an advertising copywriter. He did not become really successful enough as a science-fiction writer to stop working as a reporter and editor until 1969, four years after the publication of *Dune.* That year he returned to his home state where he was an education writer for the *Seattle Post-Intelligencer,* before turning to full-time fiction writing in 1972.

When Herbert finally ended his newspaper career and turned his full attention to fiction writing, he retreated to a six-acre farm on Washington's Olympic Peninsula, where he and his wife embarked on a kind of "Five-Year Plan" to turn the acreage into an ecological demonstration project to show how a high quality of life could be maintained with a minimum drain on the total energy system. He built, among other things, the prototype of an electricity-generating windmill that operated at high wind speeds and was fairly compact. In 1978 the federal government awarded Herbert a patent for this improved windmill design. He envisioned families using his inexpensive windmill once the cost of oil and commercial energy soared out of reach. His wife's bout with cancer stretched out the Five-Year Plan, but one reporter who visited him in 1976 said that the Herbert farm was beginning to prove itself.[7] The family was then raising enough vegetables to export a surplus to Herbert's city-dwelling sons. They raised four hundred pounds of poultry and recovered enough methane gas from the chicken manure to generate their own power supply. Of course, they supplemented this energy source with solar heating panels. He had his own small lake and grew his own wine grapes. Once, pointing to one of the many zucchini plants growing in his garden, he said to a visitor, "If God had wanted man to go hungry, he never would have created the zucchini!"[8]

And so, at age fifty-six, Frank Herbert rarely ventured forth from his pastoral retreat. Around 1980 the family established another home in Maui, Hawaii, where they spent half of the year. An occasional appearance at a book fair or a science-fiction convention was a concession to his continuing status as a science-fiction superstar, but he seems to have preferred the small-town solitude of Port Townsend, the nearest township, or the campus of the University of Washington, where he occasionally lectured. Herbert did everything he could to make his wife's last years as happy as possible. In her final days he nursed her himself, as she would allow no one else to touch her. She died on 7 February 1984 at Kawaloa, Maui, Hawaii. Herbert was married again the following year to Teresa Shackleford, his former representative at Putnam. Herbert first learned that he had pancreatic cancer that same year after returning from the World Science Fiction Convention in Melbourne, Australia, with his new bride. He was undergoing experimental cancer treatment at the University of Wisconsin when he died. He was in good spirits and working on a short story on his lap computer during the afternoon of 11 February 1986, when he complained of not feeling well. He lapsed into a coma and never woke up.

As Willis McNelly pointed out in his article in memory of Herbert published in the *Bulletin* of the Science Fiction Writers of America, it was something of the measure of his success as a writer that virtually every major paper in the country printed an extensive obituary.[9] Some dutifully repeated the AP dispatch sent over the wires from Madison, Wisconsin, but others carried a more detailed story. Even the papers of the Eastern Establishment—the *Baltimore Sun,* the *New York Times* and the *Washington Post*—carried no mere canned wire-service obits but lengthy memoirs written by journalists who knew Herbert's work well. The *Baltimore Sun*'s David Michael Ettlin headlined that a great imagination had been stilled and explained how Herbert had helped to legitimize science-fiction writing.[10] Like Ettlin, other writers neither condescended to Herbert or science fiction nor praised him beyond his merits or achievements. Herbert, a journalist himself, would have appreciated that fact.

Intellectual Background

Herbert had a wide-ranging mind that could assemble such various discourses as religion, ecology, and psychology in one consistent and highly entertaining fictional world.[11] With the publication of *Dune* in 1965, which subsequently won both the Hugo and Nebula awards, it was evident that a major science-fiction writer had arrived on the scene, and that a turning point in the history of the science-fiction novel had been reached. Herbert worked on the novel for over six years (on and off), and the labor shows in the detail he gave to his imaginary desert planet, Arrakis. Desert planets and strange customs were, of course, not new to science fiction. (Herbert had originally thought of using Mars as the location of his story, but rejected it because of the literary associations Mars would have called up in the minds of his readers. Mars would not have left him free enough to create his own world.)[12] What was new, however, was the emphasis on the formative power that Arrakis held over its human societies because of its harsh environment. The presence of ecological thinking in *Dune* made it a kind of campus cult, along with J. R. R. Tolkien's *Lord of the Rings*. By profession Herbert was no philologist, but certainly the novel incorporated a diversity of social speech types from American society at the time. Herbert's character Liet Kynes, the planetary ecologist (or planetologist, as he is called in the book), was intended to be a model of the ecologically aware person concerned with the consequences of human actions on the environment. Certainly also part of the novel's attraction lay in the fact that it dealt with areas of human behavior around which cults often form—drugs, religion, politics—together with their specialized jargons. It was obvious that such a novel could only have been written by a man with firsthand experience of many areas of human discourse who was extrapolating from current trends into the far future. This intermingling of a variety of discourses—really, he sets religion and ecology in dialogue with each other for the first time in a popular novel—was undoubtedly one reason why *Dune* transcended the sometimes narrow world of genre science fiction and reached a broader audience. And because it examined the implications of life in a desert ecology, it was able to link up with discourses current in society at the time and was hailed as an environmental-awareness handbook, despite the fact that Herbert himself repeatedly said that he was not a "hot gospel" ecologist.

Most of Herbert's intellectual contacts came through his career as a newspaper journalist, often ghostwriting for such people as the linguist S. I. Hayakawa (a man he later disliked thoroughly), or political speechwriting in Washington, D.C. It is not easy to situate Herbert on the conventional political or ideological spectrum. The only political job he ever applied for was governor of American Samoa in 1954 while he was in Washington. Herbert believed that he came close to winning the job but lost it because he was found lacking in career-mindedness. At any rate his concern with politics and bureaucracy was founded in part on such experiences. He had a standard axiom to the effect that all governments—and corporations—lie. But he was not an anarchist, or even a socialist. He did not believe in socialized industry, nor in managed economies, because governments are forced to build very large bureaucracies to manage such economies. And bureaucracies in Herbert's view were a perfect mechanism or inertial machine for hiding and perpetuating mistakes. He thought that an adjustable capitalist system was the best, but only because it eventually broke down due to its own excesses and could then be adjusted. He had an aversion for any theory that committed mankind to a single track of development that then could not be changed, and tended to scoff at planners who thought in terms of what he took to be very short-term goals. Perhaps because of the influence of Jungian psychology on his intellectual development (see below), he contended that feudalism was a natural condition into which men fall, a situation in which some men lead and others, surrendering the responsibility to make their own decisions, follow orders. He believed that this political archetype tended to recur in human history. The world of Dune is thoroughly hierarchical and based on social differences that are reminiscent of feudal times—fiefdoms handed out to dukes and barons by an emperor in exchange for oaths of fealty, codes of honor, and elaborate rules of combat—but the general aim of the Dune series was to make people *aware* of these recurring archetypes in political history so that they might be transcended.

For the most part Herbert was self-educated in such disciplines as comparative religion and linguistics. However, any discussion of the intellectual influences on his work inevitably gets back to two people who guided his reading into new avenues as well as sparked thoughtful conversation. Their names, as no others, are mentioned in most of his interviews as providing a crucial boost to his thinking. When Herbert moved to Santa Rosa, California, in 1949 to take up a post on the *Press-Democrat,* he met by chance two psychologists, Ralph and Irene Slattery. Ralph Slattery was the Sonoma County court psychologist and senior clinical psychologist at Sonoma State Hospital. Herbert described him as "a Reichian out of Freud."[13] Irene Slattery had been a student of Carl Jung's in Zurich. During the next three years they controlled his reading in the field of psychology. Irene Slattery gave him all of Jung's unpublished lecture notes to read. Because of his background in philosophy, Ralph Slattery also tried to relate psychological issues to broader questions of human existence. The names of Heidegger, Jaspers, and other existential philosophers were as likely to be invoked in his conversations as the names of Freud or Jung. The Slatterys seem to have been a very eclectic pair of psychologist-psychoanalysts who gave Herbert a crucial yet undogmatic perspective on their field. They also introduced Herbert to Zen, the teachings of which had a profound, continuing influence on his life and work. The Dune series is full of Zen paradoxes that are intended to disrupt our Western logical habits of mind. One of Herbert's favorite Zen stories concerns the postulant who came to the Zen master and said: "Master, I have come to study with you but I have brought nothing." The Master responds by saying, "Then set it down." "But Master," said the postulant, "You do not understand. I have brought you nothing." "Then take it away with you," said the Master.[14]

Toward the end of his association with the Slatterys, Herbert briefly set up practice as a lay analyst under their direction, but fiction writing as a kind of exploratory psychology was still the most demanding interest of his life: "The major reason I went into it was character analysis, being able to understand, in psychological terms, the motivation of characters. I must say it was probably the most invaluable educational experience I ever had. Everything builds upon that."[15]

Both Jungian and Freudian concepts can be found in Herbert's work from his first novel, *Under Pressure,* to the last of the Dune books. First published in 1956 under the title *The Dragon in the Sea* (the title he preferred), *Under Pressure* is a study of social schizophrenia on board an atomic subtug during a future war. With relentless realism Herbert explores the enveloped world of the submarine and its own special ecology—damp atmosphere, ever-present menace from the outside, a constant rhythm in motion like a heartbeat—and shows how this environment produces return-to-the-womb fantasies. The psychological breakdowns in the crew members are being caused by a rejection of birth (surfacing the submarine, or coming back to base after a mission) by men who have unconsciously retreated in fear to the secure world of prebirth. When asked about Freudian notions in the book, Herbert confirmed their presence, but went on to add that the book really was more Adlerian in tone, was more concerned with power and the seeking of power, a psychology Herbert found in some respects more pertinent to the modern world than either Freud's or Jung's.[16]

Herbert returned to abnormal psychology and schizophrenia in one of his last novels, *The White Plague,* the story of an American scientist whose wife and children are killed by a terrorist bomb in Dublin. Molecular biologist John Roe O'Neill is driven insane by the event. His personality splits, and a new personality driven entirely by revenge emerges, unleashing a synthesized plague that kills only women. Herbert described the Dune books, and especially *God Emperor of Dune,* as a "concretizing" of Jung's ideas about the collective unconscious.

When interviewed in *Psychology Today,* Herbert said that he was not a disciple of Jung, although he did use archetypes and symbolism, and that he developed his characters according to Jung's psychological functions: extroversion-introversion, thinking-feeling, sensing-intuition:

> Chani is feeling-thinking. She stresses those opposites. Jessica is the same. So the two dominant women in *Dune* are set up this way. And I went for other archetypal figures throughout the book. I have the young prince in search of the grail, the wise old man and the fool, the one who can say, "You're naked," to the king . . . The sandworm is the mindless monster of the deep who guards the pearl of great price. It is the black bull of the corrida, the dragon that dances in the streets at Chinese New Year. The pearl of great price, of course, is melange. It extends life and also extends the senses of the users. This gives me another chance to introduce the sensing-personality type in some of my characters.[17]

Herbert thought of science fiction, or speculative fiction, as he liked to call it, as a form of myth, but he did not see myth as absolute. Myth, and Jungian archetypes, were simply another discourse that he set out to master and that he incorporated into the dialogical open-endedness of his Dune series. In fact, what he admired most about science fiction was that it was not limited to traditional patterns of association. He seems to have used archetypes more as a strategy to get people emotionally involved in his stories than as a bedrock of human nature that could not be questioned. He believed that science fiction did its greatest, most enduring work in exposing the unexamined assumptions of our society and that an alien setting gives us a chance to look at and evaluate those assumptions from a different perspective. According to Willis McNelly, the one question that Herbert asked himself and his readers again and again in his science fiction, as if he were personally seeking the answer, was "What is it to be human?"[18] What I will show in the course of this study is the philosophical answer I think the mature Herbert arrived at through his creation of Dune (and many other alien worlds as well): being truly human means facing up to an infinite universe.

Chapter Two
Dune
Herbert's Polyphonic Novel

Dune was originally conceived as a long novel about the messianic convulsions that periodically overtake civilization and the great need people seem to have for a charismatic leader to solve all of their problems. Personal observation had convinced Herbert that in the power arena of politics/economics and in their logical consequence, war, people tend to give over every decision-making capacity to any leader who could wrap himself in the myth fabric of society. Hitler and Stalin come to mind here as this century's incarnations of the charismatic leader/hero, but Herbert's favorite examples were President John F. Kennedy and General George Patton, who both fitted archetypically into the flamboyant Camelot pattern, consciously assuming bigger-than-life appearance, where even the most casual observation would have revealed that neither was bigger than life. One of the most important themes of what later became the *Dune* trilogy (*Dune, Dune Messiah,* and *Children of Dune*) was, therefore, that one should not give over all of one's critical faculties to people in power, no matter how admirable these people may appear. Herbert saw heroes as painful for society, and superheroes as a catastrophe because their mistakes involve so many of us in disaster. But he had not yet evolved an aesthetic strategy for communicating this message to the reader through a literary work of art.

Such a technique emerged as he was writing a magazine article about attempts by the U.S. Department of Agriculture to control the spread of sand dunes along the Oregon coast in 1958. Herbert had already written several pieces about ecological matters, but his fears about superheroes filled him with concern that ecology might be the next banner for demagogues. He began to see that all of his research both into the ecology of deserts as well as comparative religions provided him with enormously interesting material for a novel if he could put the two discourses—religious and ecological—together in a contrapuntal manner, playing one against the other. What better medium than science fiction, which provides an imaginary space of extrapolation where discourses ordinarily found separate in reality can be made to converse with one another?

Gradually, after several years of creative effort, Herbert arrived at a profound reevaluation of his original concepts, a kind of crisis of authorship. He realized that he himself was just as ready as anyone to seek out the guilty and punish the sinners, even to become a leader. He realized that nothing would have given him more gratification than riding the steed of yellow journalism into crusade, doing *the book* that would right old wrongs. He needed a way to gain perhaps an ironic distance from his story's hero (who was originally Kynes, the planetary ecologist, who is killed by the desert he is trying to transform in the published version) and his adventures. At any rate, this process of reevaluation and rewriting led to the production of what I will call a "polyphonic novel" (with apologies to M. Bakhtin). Ecology was no longer simply a theme, but had become an aesthetic strategy, the author being one voice among many others in an evolving system of ideas:

> Enter the fugue. In music, the fugue is usually based on a single theme that is played many different ways. Sometimes there are free voices that do fanciful dances around the interplay. There can be secondary themes and contrasts in harmony, rhythm, and melody. From the moment when a single voice introduces the primary theme, however, the whole is woven into a single fabric.
>
> What were my instruments in this ecological fugue? Images, conflicts, things that turn upon themselves and become something quite different, myth figures and strange creatures from the depths of our common heritage, products of our technological evolution, our human desires, and our human fears. . . .
>
> Of course there are other themes and fugal interplays in *Dune* and throughout the trilogy. *Dune Messiah* performs a classic inversion of theme. *Children of Dune* expands a number of themes interplaying. I refuse, however, to provide further answers to this complex mixture. That fits the pattern of the fugue: You find your own solutions. Don't look to me as your leader.[1]

The primary theme of *Dune* is, then, ecology, and to read the book as science fiction with some estrangement and cognitive effect on the reader, we have to understand what ecology is as a science. According to Pardot Kynes, the planetary ecologist of *Dune,* the highest function of ecology is the understanding of consequences when something new is introduced into a system. One of the effects Herbert sought to study in composing *Dune* was, as I have mentioned, what happens when a superhero is introduced into society. Ecology, therefore, has a much broader meaning than the mere study of organisms and their interaction with their environments. It can mean globally social ecology, political ecology, economic ecology, and even language (as the analysis of the banquet scene below shows). What *Dune* teaches us about language, whether used artistically or in everyday speech, is that both forms of utterance depend for their meaning on an ecological relationship between verbalized text and nonverbalized elements in their context. To read *Dune* critically is to read it in ecological terms, as the text becomes the element of the environment to which the individual responds and vice versa.[2] There are only texts more or less implicated in their environments, much the same as there are no organisms in themselves but only animals that are more or less dependent on the conditions of a specific ecosystem. One of the many achievements of *Dune* is the creation of an "ecology of the word" and ecological semantics (on the simplest level, without context, this can be seen at a glance in the "Terminology of the Imperium" under *Muad'dib*). Those characters in *Dune* who are capable of exploiting the capacity of words to mean different things in different social layers of their culture, such as Paul and Jessica Atreides, are ecologists in this broad sense.

In addition to identifying the major theme of *Dune* as ecology broadly interpreted, Herbert's remarks on the musical nature of his composition tell us several other important factors that need to be elaborated on if we are both to understand and assess his achievement. If we transpose Herbert's statement about *Dune* being an "ecological fugue" from the language of musical theory into the language of poetics we can say that, for Herbert, everything in *Dune* is dialogue. In essence, from the point of view of philosophical aesthetics, contrapuntal relationships in music constitute only the musical variety of broadly understood dialogical relationships. One immediate consequence of this dialogical strategy is that the author constructs his hero not out of words supplied by other voices, nor out of neutral authorial definitions, but rather precisely out of the hero's own words about himself (which may, of course, be actively appropriated and transformed from the words of others) and his world. Herbert thus constructs not so much a mythical figure or a social type, but rather a unique character who influences the reader to accept his personal subjective image of himself. As we shall see below in the discussion of patterns of identification with the hero, it is the struggle of the hero to have the final word about himself, to escape being finalized, that is made dramatic in *Dune.* In a monological design the hero is closed, and the limits of his meaning are sharply outlined. He acts, thinks, experiences, and perceives within the boundaries of an image constructed in the world of the author. The hero's consciousness, in short, is contained within the fixed framework of the author's consciousness, which defines and portrays the hero and remains inaccessible to him from within.

Yet Herbert has renounced all of these monological premises. His heroes (or the major characters at least) all have a self-consciousness that lives on its unfinalizedness, its open-endedness, and indeterminacy. This is especially true of Leto II, the God Emperor of Dune, that apotheosis of the predator (see chapter 4). We come to feel that Herbert's hero in *Dune,* Paul Atreides, is a genuine person precisely because so much of what we know of him emerges from dialogue, yet we always feel that more will be revealed in future dialogues. Herbert's authorial position, then, is one that refuses to finalize "this complex mixture," as he calls it, or to assume a stance of authority understood in the monological sense that would deny the reader his freedoms in recreating the world of *Dune.*

Lastly, we should not seek to characterize Herbert's new authorial position negatively, as the absence of the author's usual subjectivity, as might be supposed from some remarks we have made above about Herbert's irony. On the contrary, what should be underscored here is the positive activeness of the new authorial position in this "ecological fugue." The consciousness of *Dune*'s creator is omnipresent and active in the extreme. We can find evidence of his monitoring every thematic level of his ecological novel as it developed. To his major characters, however, Herbert never attaches finalizing definitions, though he may indeed be ironic about their blindness at times; he is not creating a world of objects, but of subjects, voices, and it is through the style of reported speech he often assumes as narrator that we can feel the proximity of other consciousnesses of equal value. Thus the author is put on a level with his characters and their relationship is dialogized.

The Role of Plot and Other Elements

Because of the polyphonic nature of *Dune,* the rigorous unfinalizability and dialogic openness of Herbert's artistic world, we may wonder about the usefulness of certain categories that have long defined the literary work of art in a traditional, and largely formal, way: plot, style, setting, narrative point of view, character, genre. Scientific consciousness has long since grown accustomed to the Heisenberg Indeterminacy Principle (which plays a crucial role in the hero's prescient visions; see below) with its radical denial of absolute measurement. Moreover, in the realm of artistic cognition people sometimes continue to demand a very crude and very primitive definitiveness, one that quite obviously could not be true. This monological habit of mind is most evident in our demand for a plot summary, as if that would provide us somehow with the essence of *Dune.* In this regard, L. David Allen, author of the Cliffs Notes volume on Herbert, is to be commended for resisting such a narrow demand by showing that the plot of *Dune* can be understood on at least five different levels of rising complexity.[3]

For my part, I will provide a synopsis of *Dune,* with the added caution that the adventure plot is not the ultimate binding force in Herbert's world (dialogical interaction is), though it offers favorable materials for the realization of his artistic design. Herbert really uses the adventure plot because it relies not so much on what the hero is, his social class and family relationships, as in the realist novel, but more often on what he is not, on what (from the vantage point of the reality at hand) is unexpected and not predetermined. The adventure plot is, as M. Bakhtin points out, clothing draped over the hero.[4] What is more, the adventure plot uses any stable social localization not as a finalizing real-life form but as a "position" in a dialogue. It is true that we can understand much of the hero's character and motivation from his family relationships, and Herbert tells us that he deliberately built into the novel oedipal structures and conflicts. But Paul Atreides is also trained by nearly all of the social and political groups of the feudal and hierarchical world he inhabits, and he defines himself out of a dialogue with them and their ideologies. Therefore, plot in Herbert's *Dune* is absolutely devoid of any finalizing functions. Its goal is to place a person in various situations that expose and provoke him, to bring people together and make them collide in conflict—in such a way, however, that they do not remain within this area of plot-related contact but exceed its bounds. The real dialogical and ecological (they are practically the same thing in this novel) connections begin where the ordinary plot ends, having fulfilled its service function.

Dune opens with the Atreides family (Duke Leto and his concubine, Jessica, and Paul, their fifteen-year-old son) preparing to leave its hereditary ducal fief on Caladan, a planet with abundant water, for Arrakis, the desert planet known as Dune, formally held by their sworn mortal enemies, the Harkonnens. Both the Baron Vladimir Harkonnen and the Emperor have reason to fear Duke Leto because of his growing popularity in the Landsraad council. They have laid a trap for him on Arrakis. The Atreides family has been requested—ordered politely but without honorable alternative—to leave Caladan and take over the governance of Arrakis and to supervise the mining of melange, an addictive geriatric spice which also induces prescient visions if taken in sufficient quantities and is used throughout the Empire. While it is the planet's only product, melange is so valuable that it points to an economic promotion for House Atreides. Before leaving Caladan, however, Paul receives his first qualification as a hero when he passes a death-alternative test of human awareness, the gom jabbar, administered by the Emperor's Truthsayer, Reverend Mother Gaius Helen Mohiam.

The Harkonnens, quick to exploit Duke Leto's new vulnerable position, attack the capital city of Arrakeen with the help of the Emperor's fanatical (and supposedly unbeatable) Sardaukar troops and the aid of a traitor, Dr. Yueh. The Harkonnens bring about the downfall of House Atreides. They capture and kill Duke Leto, as well as one of his three major retainers, Duncan Idaho, a weaponsmaster and teacher of Paul. Paul's beloved Mentat teacher, Thufir Hawat, is spared because of his formidable intellectual and computational abilities (indeed, he is the human equivalent of a computer) and is pressed into service by the victorious Harkonnens. Gurney Halleck, another of Paul's teachers in the martial arts, escapes, together with the survivors of the force he commanded, eventually joining with a group of smugglers. Gurney lives and works with this group for two years, believing that House Atreides no longer exists, and that Lady Jessica had betrayed both husband and son to the Harkonnens. In actuality (although we discover that Jessica is the daughter of Vladimir Harkonnen), Paul and Jessica, now pregnant with Alia, escape into the desert where they are presumed to have been eaten by one of the gigantic sandworms that inhabit its depths.

The Fremen, fierce seminomadic warriors of the desert, capture Paul and Jessica. Using her Bene Gesserit training in muscle control, Jessica is able to overcome the leader of Sietch Tabr, Stilgar, and Paul disarms another Fremen named Jamis, thereby showing that they can be an asset to the tribe and can survive in the desert. Burning with resentment at being bested by a mere "child," Jamis invokes a tribal rule and challenges Paul to a ritual knife fight. Paul kills Jamis and receives his water and possessions. The death of Jamis initiates Paul into the Fremen, earning him his name, Muad'Dib. It also wins notice among the women of the tribe, particularly Chani, daughter of Liet Kynes the planetary ecologist, who later becomes his mate. Meanwhile, Jessica, making use of her Bene Gesserit training in the history of myths and religions, manages to persuade the superstitious Fremen that she has brought them the messiah, the Lisan al-Gaib, spoken of in their legends. Soon she too is tested, by converting the Water of Life for the tribe, distributing it among them to induce the spice orgy. This act makes Jessica a Reverend Mother among the Fremen, but it is not without dire consequences, for the baby in her womb is prematurely awakened to all of the memories of past female generations. After riding and controlling a giant sandworm, an act which makes him a leader among the Fremen, Paul also drinks the Water of Life in order to find out whether or not he is the Kwisatz Haderach, one who could tap both female and male reservoirs of ancestral memory. Paul has learned to his shocked dismay that he is the result of a millennia-old eugenics program run secretly by the Bene Gesserit, an ancient school of physical and mental training for females of which Jessica is a member. They have patiently sought power through the control of bloodlines. In fact, Jessica had been instructed by the Sisterhood to produce a daughter who, when wed to Feyd Harkonnen, the baron's nephew, would have produced this "superman" under their control. But because of her love for the duke, Jessica disobeyed. So the quest for the Kwisatz Haderach, which may be the longest single-minded project in human history, hangs in the balance. After three weeks in a coma, Paul revives but initially denies that he is the Kwisatz Haderach. Later, in the book's final scene, he affirms that he is, but it is made clear that he is no longer under anyone's control, least of all the Bene Gesserit.

Throughout all of these events, which take place over a few years, Paul is growing in powers of prescient vision. His main motivation, besides finding out who he is—a task for any adolescent—is, however, to avenge his father's murder. He wants nothing to do with the jihad, the holy war, that he can see rushing toward him from the future, but he is swept along by it anyway. The Fremen, under Paul's leadership and with the use of outlawed atomic weapons, defeat the imperial forces on the Plain of Arrakeen in a battle that blows a hole through a mountain range (the Shield Wall) and that is literally the climax of the novel. Herbert claims to have worked coital rhythms into the entire book and seems to have had a theory about war as an orgasmic experience. Alia slays her grandfather, the Baron Harkonnen, with a poisoned needle, the gom jabbar. Lastly, in a ritualized formal duel Paul kills Feyd-Rautha, his only rival for the throne on which the Bene Gesserit has placed its hopes for salvaging its eugenics program. He then deposes the Emperor and sets up a marriage of convenience between himself and Princess Irulan, the Emperor's daughter, in order to secure his claim to the throne. Irulan later becomes the official court historian. Extracts from her writings open many chapters of *Dune,* but it is clear that she never knows Paul intimately. All of Paul's children stem from his union with his beloved Freman woman, Chani.

Discourse in *Dune*

Considered formally, *Dune* employs three different stylistic templates or modes for speech inscription: indirect discourse, direct discourse, and quasi-direct discourse. With only three such templates, a great diversity is nevertheless made possible in the treatment of character speech by Herbert's habit of associating each mode with a level of conscious awareness. First, there is the authorial narration of what a character is responding to, wondering at, feeling, or considering. This mode can also range over nonverbal areas of the character's mind and may report on unconscious feelings of which the character may be only dimly aware. Herbert as narrator of *Dune* often uses this mode to develop elaborate metaphors drawn from the landscape or ecology of Dune that depict states of consciousness and modes of being. For example, the sandtrout, an early stage of the sandworm cycle, when linked edge to edge against the planet's bedrock, form living cisterns. They hold back the water in order that their sandworm vector might live. Herbert uses this sandtrout stage as an analogy for a stage of consciousness Alia can feel. Some of the ancestral voices within her mind hold back dangerous forces that could destroy her. Of course, it is not Alia who is developing the metaphor. It is not her language, though she can certainly feel the analogy imagistically. Whenever Herbert is reporting a character's inner speech directly, which is the second mode for presenting consciousness, he usually puts the passage in italics. This stylistic feature serves to call attention to the fact that the character has arrived at a conscious stage of verbalization. These passages are further identified by the fact that they are, unlike the surrounding linguistic context, in the first-person present tense. Audible speech is, of course, set off by quotation marks. It is in this last mode that we encounter the idiosyncratic aspects of a character and his/her highest range of reflective thought. In between these two modes lies the third mode for presenting consciousness, a form of quasi-direct discourse—quasi because no one actually speaks like this in real life; it is a purely textual phenomenon. Formally, it combines features of both modes, that is, it uses the language and idioms of a character while preserving the third-person, past-tense narrational context. Some linguists have called this mode "experienced speech" (*erlebte Rede*) on the analogy of listening to stage monologue in a play and trying to relate that experience to someone else. What the hero utters in the first person, a member of the audience experiences and relates in the third person. This transposition, occurring in the very depths of the experience of reception, stylistically aligns the experienced discourse with narrative. In brief, it is an aesthetic strategy for depicting the direct experience of another's speech, a form for conjuring up a living impression of that speech.[5]

In addition to these three modes, there is their interaction, as in any ecological system. When exploring the consciousness of a character, Herbert tries to create a smooth flow between these modes, so that we hardly notice that we have passed from skirting the depths of the unconscious to a level of conscious analysis. Herbert tends to use the third mode (*erlebte Rede*) somewhat sparingly in *Dune* but more frequently in later volumes. He relies most often on direct quotation, probably because he wants to make the fiction of hyperconsciousness vivid to the reader. Nonetheless the usual pattern is this: some lines telling us how the character is feeling, his/her mood, or how he/she is reacting to a scene (sometimes accompanied by metaphoric analogies with landscape or imagistic surveys of consciousness that depict subverbal reveries); then, a few brief lines of "experienced speech," often omitted in the first volume, to give us an indication that this character is about to give voice to some realization or fear; and finally, the realization itself in the character's own speech.[6]

Thus we can say that Herbert's authorial consciousness monitors and penetrates actively the consciousnesses of his characters. What is more, his own narrative voice, even when not presenting consciousness, is often influenced and contaminated by the idioms of his characters. This is most apparent in "Appendix I: The Ecology of Dune," which is devoted to telling the story of Pardot Kynes, the ecologist. It is also evident in the elaborate language Herbert devised for Dune, which he shares with his characters, and uses whenever he chooses to narrate entirely from within the consciousness of the point-of-view character assigned to a particular segment. Minor characters may be present in a scene, but their inner lives are never analyzed. What we learn of their motives comes from what they say or their behavior. The classic example is probably Reverend Mother Mohiam's long hobble through the architectural splendors of Paul's colossal keep at Arakeen in *Dune Messiah.* Although she is accompanied on her trek, the entire segment is told from her point of view and in terms of her growing sense of oppression and awe at the immensity of the place. This reliance on specific character foci is the main structuring element contributing to the narrative polyphony of *Dune.* Herbert never retains for himself an essential superiority of information. Instead he keeps that indispensable minimum of pragmatic, purely informative omniscience necessary for the development of the plot.

These stylistic aspects of discourse in *Dune* can be examined in the context of a brief passage taken from the banquet scene (Herbert himself has chosen to record this scene; see bibliography). Shortly after arriving on Arrakis, Jessica decides to set up a dinner party in order to mix Atreides officers and men with the locals on a social plane. The guests include representatives from nearly every social stratum on Dune—a stillsuit manufacturer down from Carthag; an electronics equipment importer; a water-shipper named Lingar Bewt whose summer mansion is near his polar-cap factory; a representative of the Guild Bank; a dealer in replacement parts for spice-mining equipment; a woman whose escort service for off-planet visitors reputedly operates as cover for various smuggling, spying, and blackmail operations; Esmar Tuek, a leading smuggler himself and even a man who has lived among the Fremen for most of his life: Liet Kynes, the planetary ecologist. This scene is nothing short of brilliant in the way it demonstrates the "ecological semantics" of *Dune,* especially the way in which utterances derive most of their meaning from the social context of communication in which they are produced and from paralinguistics (what Herbert, following the linguist Hayakawa, calls "metamessages"). Paralinguistics is the communication that goes on besides talk—all the pauses, grunts, sighs, facial and body movements that, it turns out, always convey exactly what we are really aiming at and are always received and (at least for most people) unconsciously understood. Jessica, however, has had Bene Gesserit awareness training and she is always using it consciously to analyze paralinguistic communication, which functions as a "context marker" to enhance or contradict spoken communication.

In addition to paralinguistics, the banquet scene is an excellent place to observe the interweaving of the two major discourses of *Dune,* ecology and religion understood in the broadest sense as a system of beliefs, rituals, and customs governing the appearance of the sacred in society. A good deal of the overt discussion focuses on the strange water customs of the Fremen and their relationship to the ecology of a desert planet such as Dune, as explained by Liet Kynes, who is himself imbued with Fremen religion as well as the science of ecology. As we pick up the scene, Kynes has just heard Jessica say, in response to a bold question by Lingar Bewt about the final dispensation of the water conservatory attached to the ducal castle, that they will hold it in trust for the people of Arrakis. Jessica says that it is "our dream" also that someday the climate of Arrakis may be changed sufficiently to grow such plants anywhere in the open. Her response has a magnetizing effect on Kynes:

> Leto's attention was caught by the expression on Kynes' face. The man was staring at Jessica. He appeared transfigured—like a man in love . . . or caught in a religious trance.
>
> Kynes' thoughts were overwhelmed at last by the words of prophecy: "*And they shall share your most precious dream.*" He spoke directly to Jessica: "Do you bring the shortening of the way?"
>
> "Ah, Dr. Kynes," the water-shipper said. "You've come in from tramping around with your mobs of Fremen. How gracious of you."
>
> Kynes passed an unreadable glance across Bewt, said: "It is said in the desert that possession of water in great amounts can inflict a man with fatal carelessness."
>
> "They have many strange sayings in the desert," Bewt said, but his voice betrayed uneasiness.
>
> Jessica crossed to Leto, slipped her hand under his arm to gain a moment in which to calm herself. Kynes had said: " . . . the shortening of the way." In the old tongue, the phrase translated as "Kwisatz Haderach." The planetologist's odd question seemed to have gone unnoticed by the others, and now Kynes was bending over one of the consort women, listening to a low-voiced coquetry.
>
> *Kwisatz Haderach,* Jessica thought. *Did our Missionaria Protectiva plant that legend here, too?* The thought fanned her secret hope for Paul. *He could be the Kwisatz Haderach. He could be.*
>
> The Guild Bank representative had fallen into conversation with the water-shipper, and Bewt's voice lifted above the renewed hum of conversations: "Many people have sought to change Arrakis."

The Duke saw how the words seemed to pierce Kynes, jerking the planetologist upright and away from the flirting women.

Into the sudden silence, a house trooper in uniform of a footman cleared his throat behind Leto, said: "Dinner is served, my Lord."[7]

The counterpoint in this passage is between those who presumably share a vision of Arrakis transformed and those who do not. The aristocrats seem to be taking sides with the social outcasts and the downtrodden Fremen against the entrepreneurs such as Bewt. Bewt has signed a contract of allegiance with the duke, but nonetheless he has considerable power on Arrakis because of his control of water facilities. He is a social climber, bold and confident enough to try to feel openly for any subtle changes in his social status under the new Atreides governance. He deprecates Kynes (who is also the Judge of the Change, one appointed by the Emperor to monitor officially a change of fief) with snide remarks about Kynes's "tramping around" with his "mobs" of Fremen. Obviously he hopes these remarks will put him in good stead with the aristocratic Atreides.

Nevertheless, and despite the social content, Herbert controls in part our response to the passage through certain features of style. For one thing, he never reports on what Bewt is thinking. Bewt is a social type, a consciousness Herbert chooses not to explore, but one that we get to know through the general dialogue. Kynes and Jessica, in contrast, are involved in a much more dramatic presentation. We know from the outset that Kynes's inner thoughts are "overwhelmed" by Jessica's remarks (which Bewt characterizes earlier and in a flowery way as "a commendable dream, my Lord") because they fulfill the words of prophecy, which are given in italics (and also in quotation marks, a stylistic feature on the significance of which we will speculate in a moment) as his own language. He then speaks directly, and oddly, to Jessica. It is up to her to analyze the meaning of Kynes's odd question about her bringing the shortening of the way.

Naturally, the lines devoted to her are stylistically more complex. They amplify her thoughts as we go through the triad of modes from her simple emotional reaction to inwardly voiced hopes about Paul. At first the narrator reports on her attempts to calm herself. Then follow a few lines of "experienced speech," appropriate since the narrator is trying, through his sharing of Jessica's language, to convey to us what it feels like for Jessica to hear such intense words uttered by Kynes. Again, the quasi-direct speech, although it takes part in the narrative context of the third person and past tense, is in part put in direct quotes, which makes it even more stylistically complex and double-voiced. Jessica searches for the ultimate meaning of the phrase "the shortening of the way," and finds it, when translated into the old tongue, to mean Kwizatz Haderach, a phrase that Herbert derived from the Kabbala of Jewish mysticism. Now, in her own language and inner voice put in italics, she speculates about the activities of the Missionaria Protectiva (an arm of the Bene Gesserit order charged with sowing legends on primitive worlds in order to aid any members of the Sisterhood who might arrive there to gain power over the superstitious), and she expresses her hopes for Paul, which also, of course, tie into our desires for a hero. As Herbert says in the liner notes to his recording of this scene: "I am showing you the superhero syndrome and your own participation in it."[8]

Besides this need for identification with the hero, which is by no means simple, recall as well that Herbert intends to show us the superhero syndrome *and our participation in it,* which implies a moment of critical self-reflection on the reader's part. It could be said, therefore, that every true reader of Herbert, everyone who can escape the monological mode and is capable of rising to Herbert's new authorial position, feels a peculiarly active broadening of consciousness. This is true not only in the sense of acquiring new objects (ornithopters, stillsuits, lasguns, the technological innovations of *Dune* as well as new human types such as the ghola in *Dune Messiah,* and all of the richly detailed natural and social phenomena on this desert planet), but primarily in the sense of a special dialogical contact with the full-fledged consciousnesses of others who are hyperaware of the world around them.

A purely formal analysis of discourse in *Dune,* such as we have provided thus far, is inadequate to deal with this phenomena of dialogical contact. Nor can it explain how the reader gets caught up in the play of voices that results from the more complicated and perhaps more fundamental situation of reported speech that is evident in the passage we have selected and indeed throughout all of the novel and its sequels. Reported speech is speech within speech. At the same time it is speech about speech. It constitutes an opening in the closed context assumed necessary for communication to take place in its "normal" form—direct communication of a message taking place between speaker and addressee in the present of a determined social context. It is the introduction of an outside, of another's words in the speaker's words, of another, often historical, context in the present context, and occurs when an utterance belonging to someone else, originally totally independent and complete in its construction, is appropriated by another person. Reported speech assumes a dynamic and reciprocal interrelationship between speaker and listener. The appropriated words may be parodied, analyzed, or otherwise modified but there is always an evaluation being made. To study the various aspects of it is to study the "ecological semantics" of *Dune*.[9]

In the formal dinner passage analyzed above, reported speech ranges from the direct discourse of the characters embedded in the reporting authorial context (dialogue in the formal sense), to their inner speech (Bakhtin's "microdialogs"), to quasi-direct forms of discourse. Yet to understand the language of this passage dialogically, to become caught up in its play of voices, is to go beyond formal and grammatical identification and to ask how, in fact, another speaker's speech is received. What is the mode of existence of another's utterance in the inner-speech consciousness of the recipient? How is it manipulated there, and what process of orientation will the subsequent speech of the recipient him- or/herself have undergone in regard to it?

The inner speech of Liet Kynes, for example, is not only put in italics; it is, as we have mentioned, set off by quotation marks. This allows it to hint at a vast oral reservoir of Fremen legends and myths, the "sayings" of the desert, which here provide a kind of ominous context for Kynes's remarks. The quotes also reveal that the voice of prophecy comes from the culturally Other. Similarly, Jessica's reaction to Kynes's reaction to her initial statement about the dispensation of the water in the conservatory, attains a multileveledness and play of intonational structures. Who, author or character, is doing the quoting of Kynes's words (from which only a phrase important to Jessica has been selected), again set off by quotation marks within Jessica's quasi-direct speech? Difficulties arise here for grammarians only. The nonitalicized form does not really contain, when considered dialogically, an "either/or" dilemma. We understand that it is precisely both author and character speaking at the same time, a matter of a single linguistic construction within which the accents of two different voices are maintained. Furthermore, these words of prophecy about the messiah are ultimately social and historical in origin, not privatized. For the most part, the boundaries of the phrase, "the shortening of the way," are preserved in Jessica's reaction, which is a kind of referential analysis. Jessica, however, cannot find the meaning of the odd phrase until she translates it into another context—the context of the Other—that of the "old tongue."

This last fact points toward the vast heteroglossia of *Dune* and toward a problem that will occupy us in the next section, that of genre. The language of *Dune* is not homogeneous, but full of the play of differences (both interlanguage and intralanguage) among various discourses and dialects. In addition to words whose etymologies are Hebrew, Greek, Latin, Chinese, or Arabic—the predominant number stem from Arabic language—Herbert even invented Chakobsa, itself a mixture of several dialects modified for the needs of secrecy. In *Dune*'s ecology language itself is modified by the needs of survival on a harsh desert planet. We may conclude by saying that any utterance in *Dune* takes shape in an environment of dialogized heteroglossia (or the primacy of context over text). The utterance, as we have seen, articulates extrapersonal forces. But at the same time it is concrete: as the expression of particular persons in nonrecurring situations, it is always filled with specific content. Thus do the words of an ancient prophecy come to be filled with Jessica's hopes for her son.

Epic or Novel?

Because of the influence of ecological thought on so many different levels, both cognitive and aesthetic, *Dune* is unquestionably science fiction. It provides us with an imaginative experience of another world which remains to provide a basis for critical understanding of our own. A much more interesting question, however, is whether or not *Dune* is the epic some critics have claimed it to be. For my part, I have already claimed, following Herbert's lead, that *Dune* is an ecological novel and that the series is unique in compositional terms. Actually, just as reported speech provided us with a means for analyzing a fundamental property of all speech acts in *Dune*—their "other-voicedness" and intercontextuality—of all the literary genres, if it is really a genre at all, the novel displays openly a diversity of individual voices, artistically organized. It is structured—or destructured—in terms of dialogue and the dynamics of narrative and counternarrative. Due to this dialogical openness and the unfolding of social heteroglossia, the representations or images in the novel are never finalized or conclusive. The novel thus defined seems well suited to the nature of science-fiction narrative, which must deal somehow with the infinite universe we inhabit. On many occasions Herbert remarked that we live in a universe dominated by indeterminacy and chance, yet our intellects keep demanding absolute truths. This concept seems to be the one recurring theme of his work considered as a whole and is a major theme in *Dune.* He defined his art as an attempt to resist or criticize this demand. It seems a bit puzzling at first, then, to discover that there are epic elements in *Dune.*

The epic, as the specific genre known to us today, has been from the beginning a poem about the past, and the authorial position immanent in the epic and constitutive for it (that is, the position of one who utters the epic word) is the environment of one speaking about a past world that is to him/her inaccessible, sometimes the reverent point of view of a descendant. Epic discourse is very far removed from contemporary discourse. There is no place in the epic world for any open-endedness, indecision, indeterminacy. There are no loopholes in it through which we may glimpse the future; it suffices unto itself, neither supposing any continuation nor requiring it. Most important is the fact that the hero is an objectified image finalized by the author from the outside.

Now we can find certain epic elements in *Dune,* but I would say that Herbert has "novelized" them, required them to lose their absolute status and interact with other elements in the process of reading. It is this process that we will now investigate, tracing our interactive patterns of identification with the hero. Herbert has always insisted on the value of process thinking as opposed to linear thinking, and so our final investigation into the ecological poetics of *Dune* will attempt to show how our consciousness shapes and is shaped by it.

To begin with, not everything in *Dune* is formulated for the reader. If it were, we would be in the presence of formula fiction. In formula fiction, according to John G. Cawelti, the most important characteristic of response is an unquestioning and escapist kind of identification.[10] Unlike more complex works of art in which readers may play a double role, at once detached and disturbingly full of sympathy and understanding, formula fiction creates a very different pattern of identification between audience and protagonist. Formula fiction's purpose is not to make us confront motives and experiences in ourselves which we might prefer to ignore but to take us out of ourselves by confirming an idealized self-image. Certainly the filmed version of *Dune,* about which Herbert expressed reservations concerning the image of the hero, is escapist in this sense. What we find in *Dune* the novel, however, in addition to the epic expansiveness of the desert landscapes and the archetypal terrors of confronting Shai-Hulud, the giant sandworm guarding the treasure, is a force of negation surfacing in a certain austerity, even, we might say, a denial of fantasy and prophecy (those two aspects of the novel E. M. Forster distinguished long ago) in the name of human limitations.

This force of negation is concentrated in the conclusion of the book (although there are strong indications of it earlier, especially in the knife fight with Jamis where our admiration for Paul as a killer is lessened by Jessica's moral injunctions). Here we can locate a sense of loss, denial, and privation underlying Paul's ostensible accomplishments. Paul has seemingly triumphed utterly over his foes, the Emperor and Harkonnens, defeating in a formal duel the only person who can challenge his right to the throne, Feyd-Rautha, and silencing the Voice that once threatened to control him, the old Bene Gesserit "witch," Gaius Mohiam, the Emperor's Truthsayer (Paul tells her that he remembers her gom jabbar; now she is commanded to remember his, 471/478). Paul has had Bene Gesserit training from his mother; this permitted him to control others merely by selected tone shadings of the Voice—now he can literally kill with a word.

Nonetheless, and however ideal the image of Paul may seem at this moment, we are reminded of the limitations of Paul's powers which result in some rather negative things happening. First of all, there is the death of his son, Leto, at the hands of the Emperor's Sardaukar troops in a surprise raid which he does not foresee. There is also the suicide death of his beloved teacher, the Mentat Thufir Hawat (Paul foresees Hawat as trying to kill him). Then there is the sense of diminishment Paul sees in Stilgar, the Fremen Naib. As Paul assumes the power inherent in his legendary name, the Lisan al-Gaib ("The Voice from the Outer World"—in Fremen messianic legends, an off-world prophet), he realizes that his powers cannot be exercised without making men into receptacles of awe and obedience to him. For this reason he finds the thought of himself as the one from whom all blessings flow—as the Fremen earnestly believe him to be—as "the bitterest thought of his life" (463/469). Also, there is the fact that the Fremen cannot know that he takes the throne in order to *prevent* the jihad, though he recognizes with a sense of "harlequin abandon" (473/480) that nothing he can do will stop any of it from happening. What we have, finally, is a hero whose powers are beyond those of normal human beings, but one who is still something less than a god. Paul's powers are always offset by a sense of the limits of his gifts.

The reader's role in *Dune,* then, goes beyond mere escapist identification with the ideal hero. Identification with the hero is merely a strategy to get us involved, a means and not an end. We are left feeling not quite easy about the heroic ideal. Great though its rewards are, it demands a price no less great. Our awe of Paul springs less from the admiration of his prescient powers than from a realization that a man can commit extraordinary acts while still remaining limited.

If we inquire into the textual bases of our responses, what we discover is a tension between two different versions of Paul, which are based on two different ways of constructing an image of the hero in time: briefly, an individual of the absolute past and the distanced image (epic and myth) and an image constructed in the zone of dialogical contact with the inconclusive events of the present and consequently the future (the novel). At the base of this tension are two different textual perspectives that are juxtaposed against each other but that are not explicitly connected. In other words, their relationship is one of indeterminacy, and we as readers are forced to build up imagistic equivalences between the two. We will come to their exact textual definition in a moment.

Every time we project an image or representation of Paul as noble Atreides and then are forced to revise it, indeed, every time we revise our expectations—as we often must—of anything in *Dune* we are forming in our consciousness what the German phenomenological critic Wolfgang Iser calls "second-degree images," in which we encounter ourselves reacting to the images we have previously formed.[11] The very presence of this impeded ideation (or force of negation as we have called it above, locating it in the last scene) in our reading of *Dune* serves to indicate that, in forming a pattern of identification with Paul, we are being maneuvered into a position outside of our habitual ways of thinking about heroes, and therefore potentially outside the time of Arrakis. We must relate our experience of the heroic pattern, and any negations of it that we may discover, to ourselves and to our own time. Remembering that Herbert claimed that he was showing us with *Dune* the superhero syndrome *and our participation in it,* we can say that it is we as readers who have to formulate the implicit criticism that lies behind these negations. It has been left largely unformulated—at least in this first volume—though nonetheless intended.

Iser's phenomenological model, the implied reader, also points out something about the process of identification with a hero that may seem obvious but that is actually of great significance to our understanding of how *Dune* communicates its meaning to the reader: we must build up an image of the hero before we can identify with him. We do this according to Iser through a series of four basic perspectives—narrator, plot, character, and fictitious reader. I have already analyzed the first three in depth, though I did not stress that the connection between them is suspended (the source of the text's indeterminacy). The last perspective—really a voice, if we want to keep Bakhtin's terminology—is not to be confused with the implied reader whose function it is to link up imagistically all four perspectives into a coherent aesthetic response. The fictitious reader simply introduces another perspective into the dynamic process. Usually this is expressed in a direct address to the reader by some fictitious voice that incorporates the specific historical views and perspectives of the society to which this fictitious reader belongs.

In *Dune* this fictitious-reader perspective comes to us primarily from the writings of the Princess Irulan, selections from which appear at the beginning of nearly every chapter and which try to establish their validity through a direct appeal to the reader. It is her perspective, temporally later than the events occurring in *Dune,* that above all give us the feeling that the world of Arrakis is epically distanced. If her perspective were the only one provided us, we would accept the illusion that *Dune* was an epic stolen from its rightful place millennia hence, since these selections tend to fix the image of Paul in an absolutely past period. In the first selection, for example, Irulan reminds us that if we want to "study" Paul, we must know that he was born on Caladan, and she gives the exact date. She then passes quickly on to her main point, which she makes seemingly from the standpoint of eternity: Paul belongs "forever" to Dune (3/3).

In Irulan's writings which are addressed directly to us as members of an aristocratic society, with all of the hierarchization of voices that implies, an image of Paul is created for his descendants. In other passages she says that it is certain that the Emperor, her father, had some of Paul's prescient powers and greatly mourned the passing of Duke Leto—fatuous claims, of course. She projects her idealized image of Paul onto a distanced horizon and in effect creates a counternarrative of events. Several of the selections purportedly come from her writings for children. They embody storybook images of Paul surrounded by his wonderful companion-teachers Thufir Hawat, Gurney Halleck, and Duncan Idaho. Thus although she was alive historically during the time of Paul's ascension to the throne, her authorial position in relation to her subject matter transfers Paul and the world of Arrakis into an inaccessible past.

In short, stylistically she writes of Paul as though he were dead and finalized. Even Paul's sayings, which are always paradoxical and open-ended, when collected and edited by Irulan only serve to objectify Paul as someone who habitually spoke by means of aphorisms. We would have to say that the valorized temporal emphasis of her writings is not really on the future. What is served in her writings is the future *memory* of a past. Certainly her writings are a broadening of the absolute past, an enriching of it, but with representations that are at the expense of contemporaneity. Irulan's world is always opposed in principle to any merely transitory past.

What happens when Irulan's perspective with its temporal zone of the absolute past and the (hierarchical) distanced image interacts with other, more "novelistic" perspectives? Nothing less than a revolution in the hierarchy of terms outlined above. When Paul and his present become the narrative center of human orientation in time, everything about Paul loses its completeness and finished quality. No final word has yet been spoken. And through contact with the novelistic present a new zone for structuring images of the hero appears, a zone of maximally close dialogical contact with readers, and their future.

As Bakhtin observed, prophecy is characteristic of the epic; prediction, of the novel.[12] Herbert on the dedication page calls *Dune* an effort at prediction. Epic prophecy is realized wholly within the limits of the absolute past; it does not touch the reader and his real time. When Herbert "novelized" the science-fiction epic, he gave to the genre a new and quite specific problematicalness: characteristic of it is a continual rethinking and reevaluating of its own premises. In addition, that center of activity in the reader that ponders and justifies the past is transferred to the future.

It would be instructive to trace in a thematic way (and something of this will appear in later chapters) the clashing and restructuring of images in Paul's own consciousness as he grapples with the paradoxes of having a prescient memory, which he eventually learns is a trap, and which does, on some level at least, finalize him. What Paul mainly learns from his prescient visions is that there is no absolute standpoint outside of time, and the illumination provided by prescience is one "that incorporated the limits of what it revealed—at once a source of accuracy and meaningful error. A kind of Heisenberg indeterminacy intervened: the expenditure of energy that revealed what he saw, changed what he saw" (290/296). Surely this is the most profound truth also for the reader of *Dune,* who must project images into the future and revise past ideation on the basis of new semantic configurations. We feel close to Paul because his struggle with time and his attempts to find a transcendental vantage point become our own in the process of reading.

One concrete example of our revision of Paul's image will have to suffice for many others that could be given. When in the third part of the novel Paul again meets up with an unsuspecting Gurney Halleck in a Fremen raid on melange smugglers, Gurney hardly recognizes him, so much has life among the Fremen and the desert hardened him. Paul is unconcerned about the number of innocent men in Halleck's group who are accidentally killed in the encounter. Unconcern is not the attitude Gurney expects though he is accustomed to the harshness of war. The upshot is that Paul is no longer an Atreides like his father who cared for the lives of his subjects. Gurney is uneasy recalling stories of this Muad'dib—Paul's chosen name among the Fremen—of how he had taken the skin of a Harkonnen officer to make his drumheads, stories repeated with evident belief by Irulan in her writings. Even though Halleck hates the Harkonnens he is uncertain about the boy he once knew. For his part Paul is glad to find Gurney, but reflects sardonically that even though he did not even draw his knife in the encounter, it will be said that he slew twenty Sardaukar with his own hands (403–9/408–14). The reader has to adjust his image of Paul as Gurney does, and we realize with Paul how quickly he is becoming a captive of his own myth.

Ecology is the major idea in *Dune,* but it is never allowed to be the hero of *Dune.* Herbert repeatedly said that he was not a "hot gospel" ecologist. His characters, in other words, were not just mouthpieces for his ideas, but had to have their own voice with which to contend with others, including his own as author. In fact, gaining control of the Voice—training originated by the Bene Gesserit—meant gaining a degree of control over others for Paul. But if this is so, what exactly is the positioning of ideas in Herbert's artistic world? First of all, Herbert rejects all absolute and idealistic ideological positions. Every idea must be submitted to the dialogic process, even the idea of ecology, and be made to interact with ideas lying outside it. Second, this ideological process is accomplished through the many varieties of dialogue in *Dune*—pedagogical, dramatic, interior—that occur between the characters. And third, it is the first sort of dialogue that Herbert altered most in revising *Dune,* or indeed rejected entirely, as is the case with figure 1, which reproduces a page from the original manuscript of *Dune.* If we bear in mind what has been said in this chapter about

Herbert's new authorial position, which he took up after a sort of crisis of authorship, it is easy to see why he rejected this passage.

To begin with, the scene as originally written approaches a sphere of ideological activity in which a monological perception of consciousness holds sway. It is a pedagogical dialogue (and there are several scenes of instruction at the beginning of *Dune*) that recognizes only one kind of cognitive individualization: error. Moreover, it in essence shows only a single mode of cognitive interaction among consciousnesses: someone who knows and possesses the truth, Dr. Yueh, instructs someone who is ignorant of it and in error, Paul. All that has the power to mean is given to Dr. Yueh. All that Paul does is ask about the number of "Lost People" (i.e., Fremen) on Arrakis. Ideas about Fremen and freedom and ecology are tied together in a purely external and mechanical fashion by Dr. Yueh. The Fremen are compared to gas molecules in a sealed flask.

If we compare this to the corresponding passage in the published version of *Dune* (38–39), we discover that what is prominent is not the idea of ecology, but the person born of that idea, Paul's "finding in these few glimpses of the Fremen a power of words that caught his entire attention" (38). Paul's questions are much more active, seeking, and alert in the final version. When, for example, Dr. Yueh mentions that the most interesting thing about the Fremen is their totally blue eyes, Paul responds with the idea of mutation. Of course, he is told by Yueh that he is in error, that the phenomenon is due to prolonged melange ingestion in the bloodstream, but still the idea of ecology—adaptation to an environment—is more of a live event played out by interaction between the two voices. Paul is hardly an independent voice in the original version; he is merely a foil for Dr. Yueh's lecture. But in the final version we can *feel* the idea of ecology, what it means to live it, for the Fremen to live on the edge of a vast unknown desert, because the idea is alive, takes shape and develops, in conversation that approaches true dialogue. The initial version expounds the prepared idea of ecology in a monological form whereas the final version shows the idea of ecology as a living image, yet the word *ecology* is never once mentioned.

Chapter Three
Dune Messiah

The events in *Dune Messiah* take place some twelve years after the end of *Dune.* The gap in time is aesthetically appropriate. Instead of presenting the vast scope of the jihad, as might happen in some space operas, Herbert chooses to concentrate on its consequences and effects. The ecological transformation of Arrakis has begun, but this seeming wealth of water threatens to destroy the traditional Fremen way of life. Thousands of war veterans now lead sedentary and dissipated lives in a sprawling suburb that surrounds Paul's massive keep at Arrakeen, having lost the old water discipline of the desert. In addition, the jihad has brought many horrors. At a conservative estimate sixty-one billion people have been killed, ninety planets have been sterilized, and five hundred others have been completely demoralized by Paul's legions. The religious arm of the Empire, the Quizarate, has helped in wiping out forty religions. "Unbelievers brought into the shining light of Muad'Dib," say Paul's priests, but ironically Paul himself is an unbeliever. He finds it difficult to believe that anyone will ever surpass his achievement. Indeed he mocks himself in public by comparing himself to Genghis Khan and Hitler.

The intensity and fervor of the nomadic desert religion we found in *Dune* has already begun to rigidify into ritual, and pilgrims from all over the galaxy flock to share in mysteries presided over by Paul's sixteen-year-old sister, Alia. Alia will come to sexual maturity in this novel and discover an ascendant desire for a mate and political power. But she has had an intensely personal knowledge of these matters since before her birth. The spice change undergone by the pregnant Jessica in *Dune* had mixed the psyches of mother and daughter, causing her to endure the terrifying experience of the pre-born. She was flooded with ancestral memories. They force her at times to think of Paul as a son to whom she has given birth. These same memories could also present her own father as a lover. Alia is the archetypal virgin-harlot, a Reverend Mother without motherhood, virgin priestess, witch, and object of fearful veneration for the superstitious masses—Alia of the Knife,

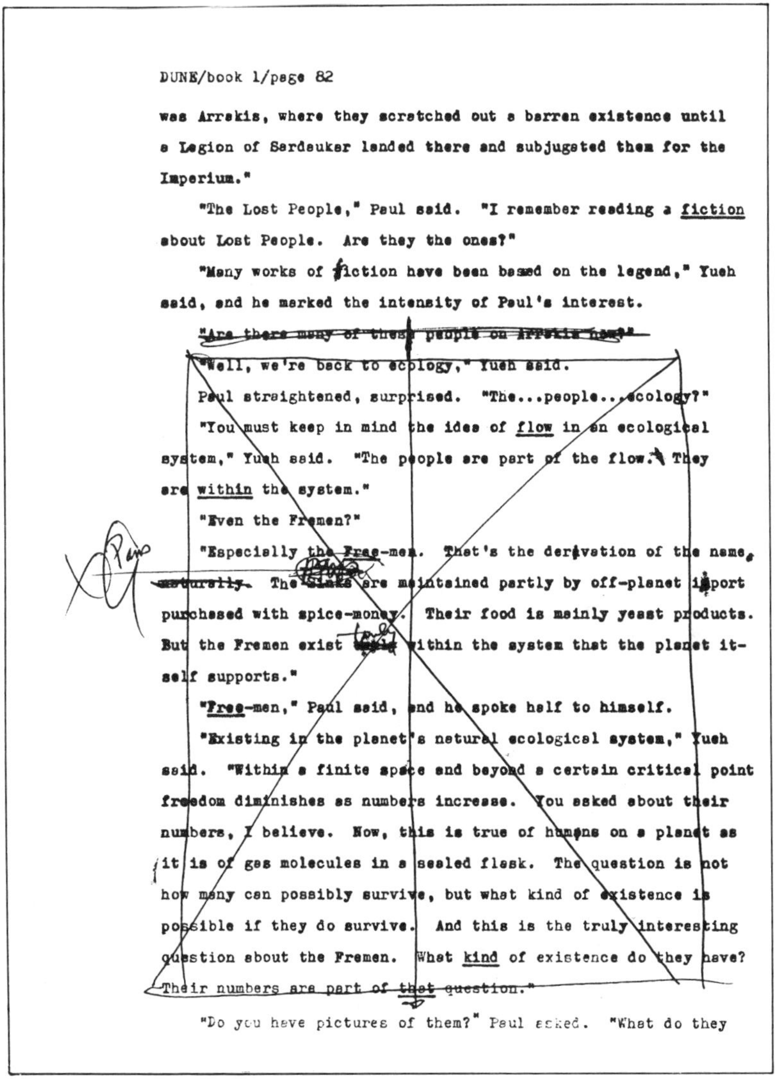

DUNE/book 1/page 82

was Arrakis, where they scratched out a barren existence until a Legion of Sardeuker landed there and subjugated them for the Imperium."

"The Lost People," Paul said. "I remember reading a <u>fiction</u> about Lost People. Are they the ones?"

"Many works of fiction have been based on the legend," Yueh said, and he marked the intensity of Paul's interest.

~~"Are there many of these people on Arrakis now?"~~

"Well, we're back to ecology," Yueh said.

Paul straightened, surprised. "The...people...ecology?"

"You must keep in mind the idea of <u>flow</u> in an ecological system," Yueh said. "The people are part of the flow. They are <u>within</u> the system."

"Even the Fremen?"

"Especially the Free-men. That's the derivation of the name, ~~naturally~~. The ~~[illegible]~~ are maintained partly by off-planet import purchased with spice-money. Their food is mainly yeast products. But the Fremen exist ~~[illegible]~~ within the system that the planet itself supports."

"Free-men," Paul said, and he spoke half to himself.

"Existing in the planet's natural ecological system," Yueh said. "Within a finite space and beyond a certain critical point freedom diminishes as numbers increase. You asked about their numbers, I believe. Now, this is true of humans on a planet as it is of gas molecules in a sealed flask. The question is not how many can possibly survive, but what kind of existence is possible if they do survive. And this is the truly interesting question about the Fremen. What <u>kind</u> of existence do they have? Their numbers are part of that question."

"Do you have pictures of them?" Paul asked. "What do they

Figure One. A page from the first working draft of *Dune*.

so called because she killed her maternal grandfather, the Baron Harkonnen, on the battlefield at Arrakeen while she was still a child. Many on Arrakis believe that Emperor and sister are one person back to back, half male and half female, "the Atreides double-being." Paul, however, wants desperately to disengage from government and religion, to stop the volcano of butchery that is the jihad, and somehow to discredit himself as the messiah of this new religion. This disengagement will not be easy. His destiny is still tied up with the fate of mankind, and as an Atreides he cannot act irresponsibly. He must also save his people.

In direct opposition to Paul's desires are the ancient power groups of the Empire—the Bene Gesserit, the Spacing Guild, and the Emperor, now represented by Princess Irulan. Together they combine with a new force (one unmentioned in *Dune*), the Bene Tleilax, to bring about Paul's downfall. Their motives for doing so are apparent: the Bene Gesserit wish to regain control of the bloodlines. Ironically the Reverend Mother Gaius Helen Mohiam's failure to admit the possibilities of Paul's being the Kwisatz Haderach had contributed heavily to the current situation. Her personal motivations in the conspiracy are vengeance and loss of power. Princess Irulan (besides being Bene Gesserit) resents the fact that Paul has made her a wife in name only. She wants to be the founding mother of a royal dynasty. The Spacing Guild, which had long maintained secret control of melange crucial to the limited prescience they used to guide ships on interstellar journeys, fears what Paul might do to the spice. Edric of the Spacing Guild, a mutated, fishlike Steersman who swims in a tank of orange melange gas, is himself prescient and can block Paul's efforts to find out about the conspiracy.

The motives of the Tleilaxu, on the other hand, are rather uncertain and are not fully revealed until the penultimate volume of the series, *Heretics of Dune.* They have important roles to play in nearly all of the later books. Tleilax is a renegade planet located on the fringes of the Empire, one which had defied the Butlerian Jihad, a much earlier holy war against computers and machines made in the image of man. The Tleilaxu are a source of immoral, though tolerated, technological products and seem eager to bring their forbidden technology back into the mainstream of the galaxy. Their representative in the conspiracy is Scytale, who seems completely amoral and bent on human exploitation, though he harbors a perverse compassion for his victim, Paul. Bene Tleilax assassins have an odd system of honor in that the victim must always be made aware of the danger and always have a means of escape, if he can but find it. Tleilaxu technology stresses genetic fabrications. At this early stage the Tleilaxu have both the knowledge and ability to regenerate dead flesh, but in later books they practice in their axolotl tanks what we would call cloning. They provide humanoid sentient tools. Gholas (the word is related to *ghoul*), sex toys, twisted Mentats, subverted Suk doctors, Face Dancers, and artificial metal eyes are examples of their products. Scytale is himself a hermaphroditic Face Dancer who can manipulate fleshy appearance across a broad spectrum of bodily shapes and features. The deepest secret of the Tleilaxu, not even hinted at in *Dune Messiah* but revealed later, is that they have been replacing their leadership with gholas, a practice which they look upon as a kind of immortality. With the exception of Princess Irulan, they are the only ones who want Paul alive, but under their control.

The Bene Tleilax know themselves unquestionably to be rivals of the Bene Gesserit, if only because they share many of the same goals. They have dabbled in various "pure essences," or human archetypes, and have created their own kwisatz haderach. But unfortunately the creature committed suicide. In secretly desiring a kwisatz haderach and Emperor under their control they are, of course, playing a double game in the conspiracy. For its part the Sisterhood is also deeply suspicious of the motives of the Tleilaxu. The Sisterhood, however, seems somewhat less cruel than the Bene Tleilax. Their genetic schemes and manipulations can be tolerated, even admired, because of their pretensions at improving humanity. Although they toy with the idea of artificial insemination of Irulan, and with the incest of Paul and Alia to preserve certain genetic markers, these tactics are ultimately rejected. Only in the last volume of the series, *Chapterhouse: Dune,* do they adopt certain Tleilaxu techniques for their own purposes, but the situation of humanity at that time is quite desperate. In *Dune Messiah* the distortions of the Tleilaxu only inspire uneasiness or even horror. The Fremen, for example, usually reject metal eyes for the blind because they feel that the user will be enslaved. In fact, they feel a particular sense of unease around the reanimated dead.

The ghola of Duncan Idaho, called Hayt, is one of these reanimated dead, and he becomes the object through which the major axes of the plot run. He serves at least three important functions. When the conspirators bring the ghola to Paul as a "gift," they are hoping first of all to poison Paul's mind with memories of old debts and responsibilities. In many ways Paul has been forced to violate the Atreides code of honor in becoming Emperor. He has willy-nilly become a tyrant and has watched his Fremen become receptacles of religious awe instead of free men. Duncan Idaho, the swordmaster of the Ginaz, friend and teacher of Paul's youth, is practically a symbol of that honor, for he died defending it when the Harkonnens took Arrakeen. As a second function, the Tleilaxu have implanted in the ghola a compulsion to kill Paul in the moment of his greatest temptation. Actually, they have mounted a two-pronged attack on Paul and Chani both, and have tried to insure that the outcome in either case will be in their favor. Should Hayt succeed, well and good. Unknown to the other conspirators, however, the Tleilaxu are harboring a deeper hope that the compulsion to kill Paul will so conflict with the old loyalties imprinted in the very flesh of the ghola that the resulting crisis will restore his memories (the ghola begins life in an innocent state, lacking the memories of the original). Once they have proven that they can restore memories to the gholas, making them even more human, the Tleilaxu anticipate having a better bargaining chip. Thus they expect to be able to offer Paul the return of his beloved Chani after her death at the hands of the other conspirators. Or indeed if Paul be killed, they will restore life to him and bargain with Alia. However, this ghola of Paul would have unconscious conditioning to make him their slave. Alia herself is the target of the third function of the ghola. Hayt is to use the renowned Duncan Idaho attractiveness to women and some additional qualities the Tleilaxu have given him—he is a *Zensunni mentat,* that is, a philosopher in the Eastern sense of one possessed of wisdom and a human computer—to seduce Alia.

Scytale is the prime mover in his plot, a few details of which Herbert gives, but whose overall shape and interconnections are left indeterminate and must be supplied by the reader. Herbert makes it clear that the plot essentially involves the attempted ghola-slavery of Paul and Chani. Impersonating the daughter of an old war companion of Paul's, Otheym, Scytale attempts to lure Paul and Chani to the Fedaykin's house. Using the dwarf Bijaz, a tankmate of Hayt's who had been prepared by the Tleilaxu for this purpose, Paul would be diverted while Chani was murdered. Meanwhile, in a developing subplot of which the main conspirators seem unaware, a Quizarate cabal led by Korba the Panegyrist (ironically also a "gift" to Paul, but from the Fremen Naibs) has a plan to murder Paul and place the blame on Chani. Paul has been making some very disparaging remarks in public about his supposed godhead. There is nothing more amusing, he says, than a Death Commando become a priest. The cabal hopes to make a martyr out of Paul and thereby insure their institutional survival.

None of these events occur in the way the conspirators hope. Scytale, in his disguise as Lichna, is detained by Paul's guards, Chani is left behind, and Paul does not die but loses his sight in a small atomic explosion caused by a device known as a stoneburner. This event comes as something of a surprise, though it has been ominously, even prophetically foreshadowed several times in Paul's visions of a falling moon which he discusses with the ghola. Indeed, the stoneburner subplot serves neither the ends of the Bene Gesserit, who need to preserve the Atreides genes for their breeding program, nor the Tleilaxu, who could not regenerate Chani from radioactive ash. It seems likely that the bomb was emplaced by agents of the Spacing Guild, who were betraying their partners—especially Scytale who would have been caught in the blast—to achieve the death of the Emperor and the advancement of the Quizarate. At any rate, Alia presides over the trial of the Quizarate cabal for conspiracy, including the stealing of a sandworm (melange is a product of the life cycle of the worms) for off-planet uses and the use of the stoneburner, atomic weapons having previously been banned by convention of the Great Houses. Paul inspires awe in the conspirators during this trial, for despite his physical blindness he can still see due to his memory of the future which appeared to him in a vision. At one point he describes to an increasingly unnerved Korba every movement, every twitch, every alarmed and pleading look he makes. But Paul sees everyone as trapped in his vision's snare. To him they seem only to be playing out their parts in a drama he has already experienced.

Next Hayt and Bijaz confront one another, Bijaz "keying" Hayt for the job he has to do. It turns out that Chani is expected to die in childbirth. Irulan has had a part in this development because she had long arranged for a contraceptive to be introduced into Chani's diet. When Chani eventually does conceive, the complications arising from this diet cause an abnormally fast fetal development. Bijaz keys Hayt to the words "she is gone," which he expects Paul to utter in the event of Chani's death. Paul then takes Chani and a large company of others into the desert, to Sietch Tabr where Chani dies giving birth to twins. By his actions, and by uttering the expected words, Paul forces Hayt to shed his Tleilaxu compulsions, break through his ghola identity, and reclaim his past as Duncan Idaho.

The moment finally arrives when Paul's vision ends, and he is left totally blind. Scytale comes into the birth chamber and, threatening to kill the twins, offers to restore Chani to Paul. But in an amazing unforeseen development Paul's son Leto II—just recently born—links with him telepathically and lends him his eyes. With this borrowed vision Paul is able to slay Scytale by throwing his crysknife. Paul resists bargaining with Scytale, but it is much more difficult to resist temptation the second time when Bijaz again offers to restore Chani. A much weakened Paul begs Duncan Idaho in Atreides battle tongue to silence the dwarf before he succumbs. This Idaho does, in effect killing a being who was his parodic double.

For their roles in the conspiracy, Korba, Edric the Steersman, and the Reverend Mother Gaius Helen Mohiam are executed on Alia's orders. Paul does not want her slain, but Stilgar disobeys. The final twist is the defection of Princess Irulan to the Atreides' side. She vows to devote her life to raising Paul's children, Ghanima and Leto. By the end of the novel, most of the Fremen Naibs involved in the conspiracy have been dealt with. The Bene Tleilax and the Guild have overplayed their hands, lost, and discredited themselves. The Quizarate has been shaken by the treason of Korba and others high within it. It is toward the remaining Fremen that Paul's final voluntary act, his ultimate acceptance of their customs, is directed. By walking alone and outcast into the desert to give his water to the great sandworm, Shai-hulud, he affirms the Fremen way with the blind and thereby insures the loyalty of the Fremen to him and his house. *Dune Messiah* ends with the observation, made by Alia, that Paul's entire life was a struggle to escape his jihad and its deification. At least, she says, he is free of it.

Although still polyphonic in structure—narrative foci are given to Scytale, Alia, Hayt, and even Reverend Mother Gaius Helen Mohiam in addition to Paul who has the largest number of them—*Dune Messiah* is much simpler in theme than *Dune*. Herbert, it may be recalled, tells us that in musical terms *Dune Messiah* presents us with a classic inversion of theme. This inverted theme is sounded at the very outset in an extract from the writings of the historian Bronso of Ix. In this, and in later volumes, the creation of imaginary texts purporting to study the epoch-making events in the Dune series proliferates. Bronso openly calls Paul's success in outwitting the conspirators and his earlier overthrow of the Emperor failures. Furthermore, Paul was not defeated by "obvious plotters," as other historians have claimed, but the failure of such an enormous and far-seeing power as Paul possessed can only be understood through "the lethal nature of prophecy."[1] The phrase in its context is deliberately left open and suggestive. Why is prophecy lethal? Hasn't mankind always aspired to predict and know the future? And how could a hero such as Paul fail at anything?

Yet it is made clear early in the book that Paul desperately wants to disengage himself from the oracle (see figure 2, discussed below). The problem seems to be that of the consequences of introducing absolute certainty into life. To know the future absolutely is to enter into a kind of living death, for the essential surprise and openness of life would be gone. Ironically, and apparently unknown to Paul, Bronso is being put to death for writing these heresies by loyal members of the Quizarate. In his death-cell interview, which Herbert indicated was to be read in the tone of voice of Dostoyevski's Grand Inquisitor, Bronso rages against the single vision that melange addiction produces.[2] The eyes of the addict are marked total blue without any contrast by the spice. The sacred spice extends life and permits the adept to foresee his future, but Bronso also points out the double nature of the sacred: it can and does take away as well as give.

In any event, Paul wants to avoid this terrible finality both for himself and his people. His final action of choosing to walk out into the desert as an outcast is intended to subvert any future attempt to assimilate his myth into any established religion. The poem that is the epilogue to the book, composed by the ghola, shows how Paul's image and words remain to haunt us:

> No bitter stench of funeral-still for Muad'dib. [sic]
> No knell nor solemn rite to free the mind
> From avaricious shadows.
> He is the fool saint,
> The golden stranger living forever
> On the edge of reason.
> Let your guard fall and he is there!
>
> (221/256)

These lines sum up much of the paradox that is Paul's legacy. Herbert's original working title of the manuscript was "The Fool Saint." Paul's sister Alia also tells Duncan Idaho that Paul is a fool for choosing to end his life in such a manner. In her view, which may be based on prescient visions of her own, Paul had but to "step off the track." What matter that the rest of the universe would have come shattering down behind him (219/254)? To Paul, Alia's mystery religion is a kind of abyss. Although he knows that she partakes of the universe that opposes and deludes him, that will never agree with any shape he gives it, he cannot entirely abandon reason for chaos. He chooses instead to "ride the worm of chaos," knowing that he is isolated in a personal sin that he can never expiate. Paul's legacy is to show us, in the image of the tragic, blinded outcast who was once an Emperor (and this is a reversal of fortune worthy of the greatest tragedy), the danger of trying to know the future. He is blinded that others may see.

The prominent motif of the eyes and vision requires comment, for it is linked to the major thematic network of the lethal nature of prophecy and the failure of vision. From many remarks in the novel, only some of which have been indicated, it is apparent that prophetic vision is a snare. Paul is already caught up in his visions before he can see. There is no neutral point of observation outside the vision. Therefore, the oracle does not so much predict the future as create it, and dictates that it follow a single track. In this sense prophetic vision is a failure, for it limits both the open-endedness of life as well as the possibilities of dialogue with others outside the limits of our own perspective. A major irony is that Paul must be blinded before he can feel the surprise of living in an infinite universe again. This surprise comes in the extraordinary scene of borrowed vision at the end of the novel, which must be examined for what it tells us about Herbert's view of the dialogic nature of human consciousness.

Initially, Paul feels abandoned in his blindness, his memory of prophetic vision having played itself out to its boundaries. He had foreseen Duncan's restoration from the ghola as well as Chani's death in childbirth and even the final outcome of the stoneburner plot. Yet his vision had contained only a daughter. Now, faced by the threat of Scytale standing over the twins with a knife, he feels another consciousness entering his own: "Paul felt himself blinking. It could not be . . . but it was! He felt eyes! Their vantage point was odd and they moved in an erratic way. *There*! The knife swam into his view. With a breath-stilling shock, Paul recognized the viewpoint. It was that of one of his children!" (210/244). A bit later, after having killed Scytale, Paul discovers the voice of his own son, Leto, addressing him:

> He turned away from them [Alia and Idaho], groping his way to a wall, leaned against it and tried to understand what he had done. *How? How? The eyes in the creche*! He felt poised on the brink of a terrifying revelation.
>
> "*My eyes, father.*"

> The word-shapings shimmered before his sightless vision.
> "My son!" Paul whispered, too low for any to hear. "You're . . . aware."
> "*Yes, father. Look!*" (211/245)

What Leto shows Paul is a staggering vision of the entire male line of which they are members. Paul sees a similar multitude of females staring out at him from Ghanima's eyes. Here Herbert is using the science-fiction motifs of telepathy and ancestral memory to point up a fundamental fact of consciousness and its relationship to social life that we frequently overlook. Herbert strikes at the heart of our individualistic culture, often a culture of seemingly inescapable solitude. Paul had thought himself alone and abandoned in his blindness, but at the boundaries of his consciousness he finds another viewpoint and another voice. Looking inside himself, he looks into the eyes of another and with the eyes of another. Paul's consciousness is once again in open dialogue with his environment.

Again this view of human consciousness as an event of interaction among consciousnesses is communicated to the reader by certain features of Herbert's prose style which operates on the threshold of two voices. In the first excerpt we find the narrator sliding into quasi-direct discourse that has the emotional tone of Paul's own language (He felt eyes!), then quoting Paul's inner speech directly (*There*!). Similarly, in the second excerpt which is stylistically more complex, representing more distinct levels of awareness, we have the same three templates for speech inscription analyzed in chapter 2, except that Leto's words in Paul's mind are put in italics *and* quotation marks, signaling that these words are indeed double-voiced and come from another. In short, we are instructed not to read Paul's inner speech as gravitating toward itself but as turned to the outside and dialogized.

In Herbert's art the plot is subordinated to the task of bringing about such tension-filled encounters where a character's consciousness is poised on the brink of "some terrifying revelation." It serves to organize the exposure of speaking persons and their ideological worlds, the process of coming to know one's language and belief system in someone else's system, which is often fraught with struggle, crisis, and, most important, surprise. This process occurred before in the banquet scene of *Dune* where Liet Kynes is transfixed by hearing the words of a Fremen prophecy suddenly fulfilled in the person of Jessica, who is so adept at improvising responses to a hostile environment. Their ideological worlds are very different. She is of the ruling class, the concubine of a duke who is the new ruler of Arrakis and Kynes lives with the Fremen outcasts. Yet they share the same ecological vision of Arrakis transformed.

In *Children of Dune* Leto II will go on to revise his father's vision, changing it beyond all recognition. And the plot arranges another important conversation between them. That seems to be the fate of prophecy and prophetic words in the Dune series: they are continually appropriated and made to serve ends that are unforeseen. But in *Dune Messiah* we also find the ghola, Hayt (who incidentally is equipped with metal eyes by the Tleilaxu), who recovers his humanity in a crisis not unlike Paul's. The importance of struggling with another's discourse, its influence in the history of an individual's coming to ideological consciousness, is enormous in Herbert. Indeed he made control of the Voice one of his themes in *Dune,* where it represents the combined training originated by the Bene Gesserit that permits an adept to control others merely by selected tone shadings. With Hayt/Duncan Idaho he seems to be pointing at the notion that one's own discourse and one's own voice, although born of another or dynamically stimulated by another, will sooner or later begin to liberate themselves from the authority of the other's discourse. This process is made more complex in the Dune series by the fact that a variety of alien voices (I do not mean extraterrestrials; there are no true aliens in the Dune series) enter in the struggle for influence within an individual's consciousness, just as they struggle with one another in surrounding social reality.

A number of discourses, professional jargons, and inserted genres, have entered into the formation of Hayt/Duncan Idaho's linguistic consciousness. In their experiment the Tleilaxu have made him a Zensunni mentat, putting together Eastern and Western worldviews. And he was a swordmaster of the heroic sort to be found in epics and romances. But in the strenuous task of overcoming his Tleilaxu conditioning, it is highly significant that Hayt breaks through to a free consciousness by seizing control of his own (or really Duncan's) voice. In the very moment Duncan's knife hand rose up to strike Paul, "he grabbed his own voice" instead of striking him (204/237). In short, Hayt/Duncan undergoes a decentering of consciousness similar to that of Paul. It is also significant that Bijaz, Hayt's parodic double, says that he does not speak but rather operates a machine called language which creaks and groans. Of course, this dehumanized and externalized image of language is what Herbert is suggesting we reject in favor of the speaking person and the drama of his/her struggle with all types of internally persuasive alien discourse.[3]

In *Dune Messiah* many things threaten to finalize Paul externally as well. Yet despite all of the conspirators, he seems aloof, even untouched by their schemes. Because he knows a good deal of what is to come, we can only assume that he plays along for reasons of his own. Paul's main difficulties in the external realm lie with forces that we have thought of traditionally as lying outside of human consciousness, in the "terrible purpose" of the racial unconscious, and in the genes themselves that have labored, apparently for tens of centuries, to achieve the brief spasm of the jihad in which the gene pool is remixed. We first learn of this "terrible purpose" in the initial pages of *Dune,* and the phrase is repeated often enough in *Dune Messiah.* Paul seems to know that the jihad has destroyed the security of the old cosmos, yet there is a deeper wisdom to the body that knows things not learned in consciousness (33/37). Along this terribly random path may lie racial survival. Consciousness, under such imperious demands for survival of the race, could lose its authentic freedom, and personality be destroyed. But Herbert does not allow biological or environmental determinism to have the final word. He preserves, as we have seen, the humanity and internal open-endedness of his hero who at the end is a tragic figure of blindness and insight. So Paul departs, having spoken his word, but the word itself remains in the evolving dialogue that is the Dune series.

By comparing figure 2, which reproduces an early handwritten draft, to the passage as it later appeared in *Dune Messiah* (38–39 in both editions), the reader can see how much Herbert worked to orchestrate what was originally in intonation a kind of tragic soliloquy into the linguistically diverse and stratified world of the novel. By itself the draft simply expresses the emotions of Paul in a monological fashion: he feels hemmed in by the boundaries of the jihad, he wants to renounce his religion and be free, to disappear like a jewel of trace dew from the morning flowers. Nearly the same phrasing appears in the final version, only it now interacts with other voices, including the author's, parceled out over two pages of text. The phrase "hemmed in by the boundaries of the Jihad," for example, is now voiced also by the author and not just Paul. In the novel this language does not represent only Paul's emotions, it is itself represented. That is, Paul reflects on his own language and certain alien words—the Chakobsa word *sietch,* which means a place of retreat and safety in a time of peril, the *adab* or demanding memory—and realizes that his own words are empty. The linguistic absoluteness of the poetic draft (no one hinders his words, no one argues with it) has been questioned in the process of incorporating it into the novel, especially by the author. Indeed, the most striking difference between the draft and the final passage is the number of double-voiced, questions Herbert has inserted: What could he answer? Could single misery be weighed against the agony of multitudes? And so on throughout the passage. The final version is fully the artistic representation of another's speech. In the process of becoming such, it has become multiaccented, part of an ongoing conversation with Chani and with Paul's own memories of earlier utterances, earlier visions. Thus *Dune Messiah*'s role in the Dune series is not just a classic inversion of theme. It begins a long novelistic process of verbal-ideological decentering that completely overturns our notions of what a hero Paul seemed to be.

Chapter Four

Children of Dune

Children of Dune opens nine years after Paul's departure into the desert. Countless dreams of power and riches now focus upon Ghanima and Leto, Paul's young twin children. In them lie temporal riches, secular authority, and that most powerful of all mystic talismans, the divine authenticity of Muad'Dib's religious bequest. Jessica, Paul's mother, had returned to Caladan with Gurney Halleck, leaving Alia to rule the family's religio-political empire as regent. Stilgar, the old Fremen Naib who served Muad'Dib and now guards the twins, is deeply troubled by the deterioration of his people as he sees Dune being transformed from desert into a water-rich planet. The great desert, which once spread from pole to pole, has been reduced to half its former size. But he accepts the divine authenticity of Muad'Dib's religious bequest, knowing that Muad'Dib lives on in the twins. Leto and Ghanima have all the memories of every ancestor. They have this pre-born status because they were genetically susceptible to melange which, taken by their mother Chani, awakened the children in the womb. Alia also is one of the pre-born—all of whom are considered Abomination by the Bene Gesserit Sisterhood because they can become possessed by a malignant ancestor. While the millennia-long breeding program of the Sisterhood produces this susceptibility, the Sisterhood also fears it because it puts an individual beyond their control. The twins, fearing that they, too, may succumb, recognize that Alia is possessed by the persona of the late Baron Harkonnen, an ancestor with peculiarly nasty habits and an abiding hatred of Paul's family, the Atreides.

The twins' grandmother, Lady Jessica, a Bene Gesserit herself, returns to Dune from self-imposed exile to find a maelstrom of plots surrounding the twins. She is driven to return by the Sisterhood, which has threatened to reveal that she is the daughter of the Baron Harkonnen, a widely hated planetary exploiter and slayer of her Duke, Paul's father. The Sisterhood wishes to learn if Alia and the twins are truly Abominations. Control of the twins' genetic lines is at stake. In this manner Jessica is herself involved in a plot against her own progeny and must find a way to abduct them so that the Trial of Possession may be administered. At the outset she realizes that Alia is truly Abomination, but the twins may not be. They have avoided heavy doses of melange and the spice trance, which they suspect precipitates possession. Alia, however, has taken more and more spice, and although she tries, she cannot see the future as her brother did. She has married Duncan Idaho, the ghola-swordmaster-mentat, who was an Atreides family retainer who died protecting Muad'Dib and whose flesh was restored to life in the Tleilaxu regeneration tanks. The Tleilaxu also gave him mysterious metal eyes. Gurney Halleck, another Atreides family retainer, is sent on a mission into the desert to find out the truth about the Jacurutu legend.

Meanwhile, on the Corrino planet of Salusa Secundus, two Laza tigers are being trained to assassinate the twins, in the hope that the Corrino heir, Prince Farad'n, may regain the throne. The tigers are being trained at the orders of Farad'n's mother, Wensicia, who is Irulan's sister. Wensicia is aided by the Bashar (a type of military governor) Tyekanik.

The people of Dune are much disturbed by a blind mystic, The Preacher, who wanders about speaking heresy. He preaches to pilgrims of the Hajj inside Alia's temple, proclaiming that the religion of Muad'Dib is not Muad'Dib and that he spurns it as he spurns them. The Preacher is led by a young man named Assan Tariq. Many believe the blind man to be Muad'Dib returned. He has issued warnings to Alia, Stilgar, Irulan, Idaho. The cult of Muad'Dib has turned sour, fermenting in Alia's mismanagement and the unbridled license of a military priesthood that rode the Fremen power. Alia fears to martyr him, but has set spies on him in the hope that he can be discredited. The Preacher has also journeyed to Salusa Secundus and interpreted a dream for Farad'n.

Leto, too, is inspired by a dream that he fears may be prescient. He dreams that he is the sun that shines out on his people. His light shines out as a Golden Path, and he wears a skin of armor that makes him as strong as ten thousand men and enables him to race across the sand dunes. In the dream he also visits Jacurutu, a sietch which has been the subject of many Fremen taboos. He sees that the ecological transformation of Dune will destroy the deep sandtrout vector of the giant worms that produce melange. This loss would not only threaten the Fremen, whose coin in trade it is, and the present imperial power, but it would also threaten the Landsraad political affiliation of Great

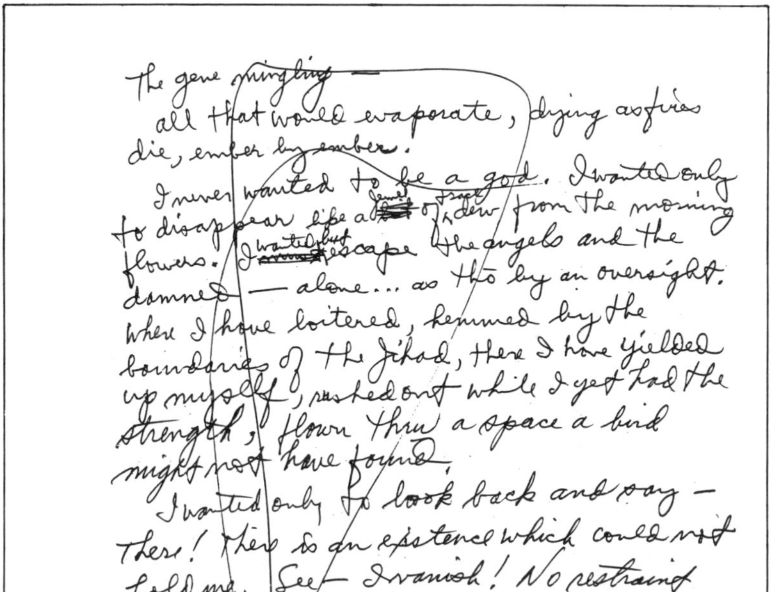

The gene mingling —

all that would evaporate, dying as fires die, ember by ember.

I never wanted to be a god. I wanted only to disappear like a jewel of trace dew from the morning flowers. I wanted but escape the angels and the damned — alone... as tho by an oversight.

Where I have loitered, hemmed by the boundaries of the Jihad, there I have yielded up myself, rushed out while I yet had the strength, flown thru a space a bird might not have found.

I wanted only to look back and say — There! There is an existence which could not hold me. See — I vanish! No restraint or net of human devising can trap me ever again. I renounce my religion! This one glorious instant is mine — I am free!

The future looked back at him out of dynasties not even dreamed. He felt his entire being cast out, crying, unchained from the rings of fate

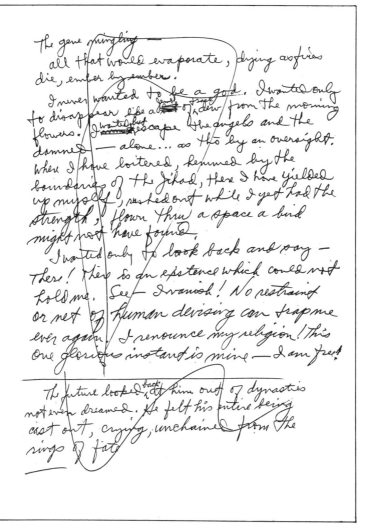

Figure Two. An early handwritten draft of a page from what later became *Dune Messiah*.

Houses, which rule on the many planets, and might damage CHOAM, the Landsraad's economic arm. The Combine Honnete Ober Advancer Mercantiles is now dominated by House Atreides, which possesses fifty-one percent of its shares. The Priesthood of Muad'Dib holds another five percent, a pragmatic acceptance by the Great Houses that Dune controls the priceless melange. Not without reason is the spice often called "the secret coinage." Without melange the Spacing Guild's heighliners—the major cargo carriers of the Spacing Guild's transportation system—could not move. Melange precipitates the "navigation trance" by which a translight pathway can be "seen" before it is traveled. Without melange and its amplification of the human immunogenic system, life expectancy for the very rich would degenerate by a factor of at least four. Even the vast middle class of the Imperium eats melange in small sprinklings with at least one meal a day. Of course, the Fremen hold the spice sacred, using it in religious orgies, and the Bene Gesserit Reverend Mothers require it to balance the multipsyche memories that their rites impart.

Trying to assume the memory-roles of their parents, Leto and Ghanima learn that the hero image of Muad'Dib must be destroyed utterly so that Leto can bring the Empire back from the brink of chaos. Ghanima is almost trapped by the inner persona of her mother, Chani. It turns out that the female psyche has more weakness in that inner assault, and in this weakness lies the reason for the Bene Gesserit fear of Abomination. Leto can certainly feel the power of his father's will, but Paul voluntarily withdraws, for he knows that *any* possession, even that of Paul with his son against their enemies, reduces the possessed to Abomination. Leto is weakened, as Paul was, by the uncertainties of his situation. He is tempted to use melange, knowing that his flesh has the ability to transform it into a vision of the future. Yet his flesh also wears the deep knowledge learned in blood by Paul. Those who seek to know the future instead find themselves trapped into a lifetime whose every heartbeat and anguished wail is already known. Paul's final vision about "the golden genesis" of man, we are told, had shown the precarious way out of that trap, and Leto now knows that he has no other choice but to follow that way.[1]

Leto then upsets Stilgar by forcing the old Fremen to question traditional values. Leo tells Stilgar that he (Leto) is called upon to reduce his father to human stature, to undeify him. He points out that he himself is abrim with innate knowledge, with memories of traditions more ancient than Stilgar could imagine, all of them resisting change.

And yet, gesturing at the Shield Wall shattered by Paul's Fremen, he reminds Stilgar that his father had changed all that. Like the traditional Fremen, Leto is past-directed, but he wants to overcome the inertia of the past. For Stilgar the Fremen cave warren, the sietch—the word means a place of sanctuary in a time of trouble—was a model for all thinking. For him a sense of enclosure should pervade every individual choice, should fence in the family, the community, and every step taken by a proper government. The model of the sietch even has its counterpart in the sand: Shai-Hulud. The giant sandworm was surely a most formidable creature, but when threatened it hid in the impenetrable depths. Stilgar tells himself that change is dangerous, yet he recognizes that planetary serfdom had reached its peak on Arrakis. The Fremen had turned inward, barricaded in their minds as they were barricaded in their caves. He realizes that the very meaning of sietch had been perverted on Arrakis into a monstrous confinement for an entire population. In the end he feels lost, his old beliefs crumbling. Leto's new outward vision, something that Paul had willy-nilly created, produced life that desired to move away from containment. Tradition is no longer the absolute guide Stilgar thought it was.

Alia is growing more insane with each passing day and believes that all sorts of plots are being hatched against her. Duncan Idaho tries to convince her that the plots are directed against the twins, but Alia insists that she is the target. This belief is shared by Irulan, the Corrino family princess who was Paul's wife, but not mate. Alia orders Idaho to abduct Jessica, making it appear an act of House Corrino. Leto, learning of the plot, orders Jessica to allow the abduction. Jessica, knowing that Leto and Ghanima can manipulate people thus, sends her trusted aid Gurney Halleck to trap Leto and subject him to a perilous training. Seeing at last that Alia is possessed, that she has taken Javid, the leader of her Society of the Faithful, as a lover, Idaho agrees to the abduction but secretly vows it will be done his way and not as Alia orders. In his pain and anguish over what has happened to Alia, he finds that Tleilaxu metal eyes are not immune to tears.

As the novel reaches its mid-point crisis, Jessica accepts Alia's invitation to attend the Regency Council and judge the supplicants, although she suspects it is a plot to discredit her. One supplicant is Ghadhean al-Fali, an old Naib who speaks as one of Muad'Dib's Fedaykin death commandos. Ghadhean al-Fali pleads that the ecological transformation that is to make a water-rich paradise of Dune is also destroying the giant worms that produce the spice. As al-Fali demands his Fedaykin right of audience, one of Alia's priests tries to assassinate Jessica with a maula pistol. Al-Fali kills the priest and, with Jessica, escapes the audience chamber, fleeing to one of the old sietch hideaways.

Meanwhile, the twins decide on their own to go secretly to the desert outcropping called The Attendent. They carry Fremen gear and the baited robes, sent to them as a gift by House Corrino, that will bring the Laza tigers to attack them. While Jessica waits at the Red Cavern Sietch with her Fedaykin supporters, a small-scale civil war breaks out between the desert Fremen and the Imperial Military Fremen who are loyal to Alia, but it settles quickly into an uneasy truce. The Fedaykin know that they are under an official report of crimes against the Imperium. Alia takes the official tack that her mother has been suborned by enemies of the realm, although the Sisterhood has not yet been named. The high-handed, tyrannical nature of Alia's power is now evident, however. Jessica sends a direct and simple message to Stilgar: My daughter is possessed and must be put to the Trial of Possession. But Duncan Idaho arrives as though he were a messenger from Stilgar and abducts Jessica, saying that he does the Preacher's bidding. He takes her a prisoner to Salusa Secundus, where Farad'n, fascinated by Atreides' history and religion, accepts Jessica as a teacher. She is ordered to train him as she had Paul, but Farad'n is bargaining for the time in which his Sardaukar legions can grow stronger and the Fremen weaker.

Back on Arrakis, the twins walk in the desert to The Attendent and see the Laza Tigers come to attack. Fleeing, they run toward a small crevasse in the basalt of an outcropping, knowing that the crisis of the attack will focus there. Ghanima is injured as they reach the narrow place where they can escape the Laza Tigers. Leto kills one of the tigers with a poisoned crysknife. Although injured, Ghanima insists on taking the second tiger but her arm is severely mauled. She kills the tiger. Ghanima goes back to Sietch Tabr under a self-induced hypnotic compulsion that Leto is dead. She can be released from her compulsion only by the ancient words *Secher Nbiw,* or Golden Path. Ghanima truly believes that Leto died saving her, and she is prepared to pass any test administered by Truthsayers. In reality her brother summons a worm that devours the bodies of the tigers and that he rides off into the desert to Jacurutu, also known as Fondak. It is peopled by Fremen outcasts, a tribe believed to have been wiped out long ago because they killed any traveler to obtain the water of his flesh. When she reaches Stilgar's sietch, Ghanima discovers the traitor who had directed the Laza Tigers, Palimbasha, and slays him with a makeshift blowgun, a device she recalls from her ancestral memories. Everyone believes Leto dead, and Ghanima ends up in Alia's keeping as a quasi-hostage.

Returning to Salusa Secundus, we learn more of Farad'n's character and the devious plottings of the Bene Gesserit. Farad'n is fascinated with the uses of power, with Muad'Dib, Arrakis, the Fremen, and their religion. He secretly admires House Atreides. Seeking to emulate Paul Atreides, he is spice-addicted and pours over the family's history. Wensicia has had Tyekanik lead Farad'n into the Arrakeen religion, but when she finally reveals all of her plotting on her son's behalf, he resents the manipulating of his life and is disgusted with how the Laza Tigers were trained, by letting them kill children who looked and were dressed like the twins. He is, however, not displeased with the outcome, since with Leto seemingly dead, the way to the imperial throne seems clear. Farad'n finds he can play mind games better than his mother, can lead her around and force her to expose her inner thoughts. He agrees to have her banished in punishment for her role in the plot against the twins. Jessica has demanded this in exchange for the Bene Gesserit training he dearly wants. For their part and unknown to Jessica, the Sisterhood has promised to put Farad'n on the throne with Ghanima as his mate. They have not abandoned the Atreides line, but still want a kwisatz haderach under their control. They have invested too much in the long breeding program. They want an open clash between Atreides and Corrino, a situation where they can step in as arbiters and from which they will emerge with control of both Ghanima and Farad'n. In effect, sending Jessica to Arrakis has been a classic delaying action in the Sisterhood's traditional pattern of not seeking power openly—a reasonable story because it squares with what one might believe of their motives and concerns about Abomination. But they want Jessica out of the way. She is a flawed sister who had failed them once before by bearing a son to Duke Leto.

The scene shifts again to Dune, where Leto, having dismounted the worm and having dug himself into the sand, is following the trail of his own future visions. Leto has not told Ghanima all of his vision nor the reasoning derived from it. To turn his back on his father is like betraying a god to Leto, but he now realizes that he must discredit his father's memory and follow his own dream-vision because the Atreides Empire has fallen into the worst of times. What is more, the universe at the moment being locked into Paul's vision, Paul must somehow still be alive. Leto feels his own vision to be contained within his father's as a peculiar sort of doubled vision. He resolves to make mankind experience the alternative to Muad'Dib—the Golden Path which Paul himself had glimpsed but turned away from—though it may hate him for doing so, and to make it understand the nature of its own myths of security and certainty.

Concurrently, in Arrakeen, The Preacher comes to Alia's temple plaza on the day of the Kwisatz Haderach, the first Holy Day of the faithful who follow Muad'Dib. It is the twenty-eighth day of official mourning for Leto. Alia, disguised, waits with the throng in the plaza, seeking to discover if this Preacher is really her brother. The Preacher demands to know if the moral suicide of all men is the inevitable aftermath of a messiah. Because of the power of his voice, Alia wonders if he might not be Bene Gesserit-trained, and thus another ploy in the endless power game. By attacking Alia's priesthood, The Preacher gains the crowd's sympathy and holds it. He tells them that the established religion has turned them into placid cattle, whereas the message of Paul's life—and Leto's as well—is to abandon certainty. He tells them that mankind is a probe into the uncertain, even the unknown. At the end, he leaves, after identifying himself to Alia. It is Paul-Muad'Dib. Alia, her universe tumbling about her, stands intoxicated with despair, unable to move. For the first time we truly pity her. She is a victim whom everyone has abandoned.

On Salusa Secundus, Jessica awaits Idaho in her quarters at Farad'n's Keep. Knowing that spies watch, she speaks accusingly to him. Shocking Jessica, Idaho says he is there for the same reason she is. Idaho speaks of Fremen who now curse House Atreides. There is talk of a peace-bringing marriage between Ghanima and Farad'n. In this scene Duncan sets the stage for a formal withdrawal from Atreides' service. Jessica wants Idaho to serve her own designs, but wonders if she might have to kill him. She makes a move in that direction, but Idaho reads her intentions in her actions. He forces her to accept his withdrawal from Atreides' service. Idaho departs, accusing her of being a Bene Gesserit witch working for the Sisterhood, not for the Atreides.

On Arrakis, Leto comes to the Iduali sietch—Jacurutu/Fondak. He waits, hidden in the desert during daylight, watching that mysterious place where not even a sentinel carrion bird waits. A great sandstorm is coming. Leto feels a strange resonant relationship with the taboo of this place because he has refused to be confined in the system that his ancestors bequeathed to him. As he tries to enter the sietch, where he senses his Golden Path is to begin, a trapvine catches him and he is taken captive inside. His captor, later revealed to be Gurney Halleck, reveals that he is the one for whom the trap was baited. Halleck tells Leto that he must be educated, that now he is just a repository for all those dead lives and has no life of his own as yet. At Arrakeen, however, Alia's guards miss capturing The Preacher and the attempt, forbidden by Alia, arouses her to rage. The Baron's persona possessing Alia reminds her that Ghanima's knife is sharp and might yet cut Alia out of her predicament.

At Jacurutu, Namri, father of Javid and a descendent of the Iduali, identifies himself to Leto. He says he is Leto's teacher, there to test. Namri plays an ancient riddle game with him, a game in which the wrong answer means death. Leto recognizes Namri as a human gom jabbar in the service of the Bene Gesserit who are testing his right to be called human. On Salusa Secundus, Farad'n also begins his Bene Gesserit education under Jessica who starts him with elementary lessons in patience and in how to achieve a relative stability in the face of a constantly changing nature—which they call the Ultimate Non-Absolute. Leto is told by Gurney Halleck that his education also has been planned to the last detail. Halleck injects Leto with spice essence against his will, and Leto begins a long "worm trip," in which he must face Abomination, prescient trance, and all of the things he and Ghanima fear most. In this first melange overdose Leto experiences multiple futures, including one in which his skin is not his own. He feels himself survive the coriolis storm which no flesh has ever endured. He sees the multidimensional relief map of his own future. He lets his awareness flow with the terrifying visions, which also involve the past and the now. With the help of an ultimate ancestor, one who is greatest within him, named Harum, he dominates his inner lives. Now he has multipasts, multifutures, but he seeks only one future—his vision of the Golden Path. Leto's mass experience of his ancestors is so powerful that, when aroused, it could subdue a nation, a society, or an entire civilization. He realizes that no one can ever be allowed to see this power within him, not even Ghanima. Leto's vision is a glimpse of the flowing infinity that is the universe which cannot be forever ordered and formulated. He realizes that there is no single set of limits for all men and understands the limits of prescience. Universal prescience is an empty myth. Only the most powerful local currents of time may be foretold. But in an infinite universe, local can be so gigantic that the mind shrinks from it. Leto tells Namri that there was no moral grandeur to his father's life, only a local trap which he built for himself.

At the same time, on a more mundane level, Alia is seeking the betrothal of Ghanima to Farad'n in the knowledge that Ghanima will kill Farad'n, precipitating a crisis out of which she can emerge victorious. Ghanima, believing Farad'n to be the author of Leto's assassination, defies all inducements to the betrothal, then accepts with the reservation that she will kill Farad'n. Alia wants Ghanima to accept as a trap for Farad'n, kill him, and thereby destroy all trust in Atreides' honor and in Paul's prophethood. Irulan protests that such a false betrothal will invoke the wrath of all the Great Houses and possibly cause the downfall of the Empire, but Alia is unswayed by her concern, which is mainly for Paul's memory and his children whom she truly loves. She cannot, however, understand Ghanima's bloodthirstiness, nor the ancient sense of vendetta that hangs like an aura around her, but Irulan is not Fremen. Fremen children were accustomed to slay the wounded on the battlefield, releasing women from this chore so that they might collect the bodies and haul them away to the deathstills.

After a vision in which the eco-language of Dune rages through his mind on its wings of music, Leto finds an inner balance that reflects upon the universe and returns him to an image of calm strength in which he can seek his Golden Path. Leto finds the clue to that calmness in the Missionaria Protectiva of the Bene Gesserit, who knew how to manipulate people and religions. In high spirits he points out to his tormentors, Halleck and Namri, that they are seeking something from him that he cannot give, that is, absolute judgments. He tells them that every judgment teeters on the brink of error, and that to claim absolute knowledge is to become monstrous. Knowledge is rather an unending adventure at the edge of uncertainty. In effect, Leto begins to test them and their beliefs, to manipulate them. He tells them that he has not only showed them his faith, but that he has also made them conscious of their own existence through their inquisitions and dialogues: "Life requires dispute. You've been made to *know*—by me!—that your reality differs from all others; thus, you know you're alive."[2] Leto also tells them that he brings the act of ultimate self-examination to humankind, the *amor fati*. The two men are made uneasy by Leto's ability to find such loopholes in their interrogations, and they go off to reflect, but not before Leto says he will cooperate with his grandmother and the Sisterhood. It is clear that Leto is well on his way to becoming the most treacherous being in the universe, the God Emperor of Dune. After Halleck and Namri depart, Leto reaches the new higher level of awareness that the Bene Gesserit has sought for millennia. He perceives the structures of imperial society and their communities and grasps the archetypes that have haunted his assumptions, the myths and languages that have hemmed him in. He now looks upon mankind as a colony organism that he can teach an oppressive social order over thousands of years. He promises within himself to bring mankind thousands of years of social order, but not the kind they expect. He addresses his father-within and says that they together (or perhaps Leto is already using the royal "we") will give humanity "question marks," complexities to occupy their minds, until they learn how dangerous he really is.

While Farad'n achieves the first learning steps in Jessica's Bene Gesserit teachings—how his mind controls his reality and *prana-bindu* muscle control—Leto pursues his vision of the Golden Path. He sees the green burgeoning future of Arrakis, which also marks the end of the worms, the end of melange, and the end of power for those who now hold it. He knows that he is submitting more and more to the onslaught of those collective lives whose memories once made him feel he was real. He has sought power in the reality of his trances, but these trances are fantasies in which he has escaped from the fear of Abomination. He struggles to find a center from which he can watch without purpose the flight of his visions, of his inner lives. Once he accomplishes this new position of consciousness, he finds that his memories no longer invent the next moment for him. They merely show him how to create new moments. Leto's multitude of inner lives fall into alignment, nothing tangled or mixed, but it is neither a victory nor a defeat. They become silent as he addresses them all saying that only through him will they, and mankind, achieve the only way out of chaos: understanding through living. He tells Sabiha, Namri's niece who is also there to guard him, that unless the dance of life on Dune is restored, the dragon on the floor of the desert will be no more, that he is a living glyph to write out the changes that must come to pass. Those changes will require him to do brutal things, to go against his most basic, dearest wishes. He might have to kill a friend or give his sister to a monster.

For her part, Ghanima fears that Alia's fate, Abomination, may be her own. Arguing with Irulan, Ghanima reminds her that the Atreides have a bloody history that stretches back to Agamemnon. When Irulan comforts her, Ghanima hopes that she will not have to kill Irulan. Leto, however, does not know whether to be thankful to his grandmother or to hate her. It is becoming evident to him that the Bene Gesserit intend to restore Pharaonic Imperialism through him, forcing him to marry his sister. Jessica had wanted him to have conscious-level instincts. But instincts, he now understands, are only racial memories of how to handle crises. His direct memories of other lives tell him far more than that. His real problem is not to reveal himself to Gurney or to Namri. Also, Leto has had a sexually potent vision of himself and Sabiha entwined together in an alternate future. It would be sweet to allow this future to come into existence, but Leto resists the temptation. Sabiha feeds the spice essence to Leto. One future links Leto to Sabiha, another future endures for thousands of years and his skin is not his own. Leto, although weak from the spice trance, overcomes Sabiha and escapes into the desert. Namri gloats that Leto's stillsuit has been disabled and the boy will die without water. A coriolis storm is coming.

Idaho returns to Alia and reports that Jessica is training Farad'n in the Bene Gesserit Way. Alia is angry and incredulous. Idaho retreats into mentat coldness to preserve his own balance, a mask for the raging grief that threatens to engulf him at the knowledge of what his beloved has become. Duncan is sent to Sietch Tabr, where Irulan and Ghanima are under Stilgar's keeping. Javid, Alia's lover and a secret agent of Jacurutu, is there negotiating an uneasy true with wild Fremen tribes who have smashed the qanats and spilled their waters into the sands. The Kagga Basin is alive with sandtrout that are reaping the water harvest. (Sandtrout are water scavengers that are the larvae form of the sandworm; they attach to one another and wall off water from the surrounding environment, forming a nest site, sometimes called a prespice mass. These masses later explode, exposing the chemicals of the nest site to the sun and air. Melange is the end product of this process.) Duncan takes off without Alia's trusted Amazon aide, Zia, realizing mentat-fashion that Alia intended him to have a fatal accident.

In the desert Leto knows that he must cut the threads of his vision of Sabiha and seek out his father, The Preacher. He deliberately avoids doing what these other visions have shown him. He goes to the Tanzerouft, the Land of Terror: thirty-eight hundred kilometers of wasteland nearly untouched by the work of the ecological transformation remaking Arrakis. Nowhere has a vision seen him fleeing Jacurutu this way. Leto rides a giant worm south into the storm and there burrows into the sand, seals himself into an airless tent, gambling to survive by using ancestral memories to achieve a trance that will virtually reduce his oxygen needs to zero. In so doing, he commits himself to the unknown. Whatever happens, he knows that he must break the threads of the other visions, leaving him at last only the Golden Path.

On Salusa, the Bene Gesserit training works its magic upon Farad'n. Jessica tells him that Paul did not really see *the future,* but rather the process of creation and its relationship to the myths in which men sleep. She explains the Bene Gesserit view of molecular memory expressed as ritual, and provides him with the most crucial of all Bene Gesserit observations: life is a mask through which the universe expresses itself. Jessica is very pleased with her student. Farad'n graduates. He is no longer Corrino; he is now Bene Gesserit.

Leto awakens in the oxygen-starved darkness of his stilltent and digs his way to the surface. Looking out at the night constellations and the desert, he realizes that, seen close up, the universe is a hustling place like the sand all around him, a place of uniqueness and change. Seen from a distance, however, only patterns lie revealed and those patterns tempt one to believe in absolutes. He reflects that in absolutes we may lose our way. Patterns may guide or they may trap. One has to remember that in an infinite universe patterns change. Leto takes another worm and rides further south searching for the sietch of Shuloch, the real core of those who escaped Jacurutu. On the way he thinks of this passage as a new ceremony for his life, recognizing that he will have to adopt many new ceremonies to keep his personality from dividing into its memory parts, "to keep the ravening hunters of his soul forever at bay. Contradictory images, never to be unified, must now be encysted in a living tension, a polarizing force which drove him from within" (311/308). The metaphor of encystment is an ecological one, since Leto knows that the sandtrout, introduced to Dune from somewhere else long ago, encysted the available free water and made Dune a desert planet . . . and they did it to survive (40/32). In a planet sufficiently dry they could move on to their sandworm phase—and this is what Leto intends to do too, although it is not revealed at this point in the story.

At Shuloch, Leto overcomes Muriz, the father of Muad'Dib's guide, Assan Tariq, and one of the Cast Out. Leto forces the man to taste his own blood (sharing water), thus insuring the countenance of Shuloch's leaders, and becoming part of the "Spirit River" at Shuloch. Later, he plays on the man's superstitions and fears that the ecological transformation will destroy the worms and leave all Fremen destitute. It turns out that Shuloch is a kind of sandtrout fishery. The smugglers have set up holding pens to catch the sandtrout, who are attracted to the water in the qanats. They are selling the sandtrout and worms to off-planet customers. Sabiha is also at Shuloch. Leto tells her that she is the fate of his vision. His eyes brimming with tears, Leto tells Muriz mysteriously to pray for Kralizec, the battle at the end of the universe.

Meanwhile, at Jacurutu, Halleck and Namri quarrel. Namri reveals himself as Alia's servant and tries to kill Halleck, but Halleck slays him. The scene then shifts quickly back to Shuloch, where Leto realizes that Sabiha, although she has prescient visions, depends upon absolutes and cannot handle the rigors of terrible decisions he must make because he is a membrane that registers infinite dimensions. Leto decides that now is the time to shift to his own vision. At night he goes out to the qanat where the sandtrout swarm and allows them to encyst his body as a living skin, hoping that the Golden Path will emerge from his ordeal. The membrane works precisely as his vision had predicted, enabling him to leap into the air and speed across the sand with amplified strength. Thus the first step on the Golden Path, making his skin not his own, is accomplished. Leto then faces the second major step and walks out into the desert to see if the worms will attack him. But the worms will not attack the deep-sand vector of their own kind. In fact, Leto can almost command the worms. He leaps for joy in manic exhilaration, racing across the dunes. His sensuous joy in his new amplified muscles creates a ballet on the desert, a defiance of the Tanzerouft that no other has experienced ever. Here is the great leap onto the Golden Path at last! Leto has put on the living, self-repairing stillsuit of a sandtrout membrane, a thing of unmeasurable value on Arrakis . . . until one understands the price. Leto is no longer human, and will live for thousands of years as he adapts to the sandtrout skin and it to him, creating a strange and terrible incarnation. He has embarked on a path of no return and can never regain his humanity. Leto goes off into the desert to smash the qanats. In a month of this activity he plans to set the ecological transformation of Arrakis back a full generation, to give himself space to develop a new timetable. Leto has prepared a trap in time and space as an unforgettable lesson for himself and all of mankind. Yet he knows that he still must confront and dispute with his father so that only one vision will emerge.

Once again the plot has worked to arrange a dialogue on which the fate of the universe hangs. Leto easily commands a worm, riding northward until he encounters The Preacher on his way to Shuloch. Leto's long dispute with The Preacher is arguably the single most important conversation in the Dune series, so far-reaching are its implications. It manages to redefine everything while remaining open-ended. The Preacher is in fact Paul Atreides, but we are told that Paul had passed from the universe of reality into the *alam al-mythal* while still alive, fleeing from this thing his son had dared. We do learn that Paul had seen Leto's Golden Path and rejected it in horror, for he did not want to give up his humanity. At any rate the Preacher tells Leto that he is not his father, only a poor copy, a relic. Nonetheless, a battle of visions takes place. Each of them has only a desperate and lonely courage upon which to rely, but Leto possesses two advantages: he has committed himself upon a path from which there is no turning back, and he has accepted the terrible consequences to himself. His father still hopes there is a way back and has not made a final commitment. Leto makes it clear to The Preacher that he has no passionate belief in truth, no faith other than what he creates. By such beliefs he will post the markers of the Golden Path showing others how to be human, though it is ironic that he himself will not be human. True to his orders from the Cast Out, Assan Tariq tries to kill both Atriedes by summoning a worm, but Leto kills him despite The Preacher's plea for mercy. This act of killing The Preacher's guide precipitates the father's defeat. But he is still defiant. Blind, angry, and near despair as a consequence of his flight from the vision that Leto has accepted, The Preacher once again seems like Paul Muad'Dib. Leto proclaims that now he is Paul's guide, but Paul rejects him, asking Leto whether he knows the universe he has created. Leto responds by saying that he is there to give purpose to evolution. Paul says, "This is your universe now" (349/346). Paul has tried to guide the last strands of a personal vision, a choice he had made years before in Sietch Tabr. For that, he had accepted his role as an instrument of revenge for the Cast Out, allowing them to ply him with spice essence and women while at the same time baiting Alia, tempting and confusing her into inaction and the wrong decisions. It saddens Leto to learn that his father has accepted all this degradation rather than choose Leto's view, which involves thousands of years of enforced dormancy and stagnation to teach humankind a lesson it will never forget. He freely admits, though, that his vision is not one whit better than Paul's. Worse, perhaps. Paul's jihad will be a summer picnic on Caladan compared to Leto's Kralizec. But it is made very clear that Paul's choice was a personal one that he did not take far enough. Kralizec, the Typhoon Struggle, is necessary. It is either that or extinction for mankind. Leto thinks on a time scale entirely different from his father, and he is not much troubled by what he anticipates will be the reaction to his reign: "For a time they'll call me the missionary of *shaitan,* . . . then they'll begin to wonder and, finally, they'll understand" (351/349). Leto may indeed become the missionary of Satan, but Paul acknowledges the greater breadth of his son's vision. He had said himself that Muad'Dib, the Hero, must be destroyed.

The last fifty pages of *Children of Dune* are packed with dramatic events. At Sietch Tabr, which is supposedly neutral territory, Duncan Idaho kills Javid, thereby ending his cuckoldry, and, provoking Stilgar into killing him, dies a second death for the Atreides. Stilgar, expecting Alia's revenge, goes over to the rebel side and escapes into the desert with Ghanima and Irulan. Back in Arrakeen Alia appoints Buer Agarves, the grandson of Stilgar's cousin, head of a search-and-destroy mission while also taking him as a lover. Gurney Halleck links up briefly with smugglers at Jacurutu, just long enough to steal an ornithopter. Several months pass in which Leto, "the Desert Demon," destroys more and more qanats, spilling their waters into the sand. His random depredations make home-guard duty the first concern of Alia and the Naibs. Stilgar, in fact, enjoys his role of "will-o'-the desert" because it permits the return of some of the old Fremen ways. Nonetheless, the worms are dying, and the price of melange has risen drastically. Ghanima wonders where help is to be found. During a negotiating visit from Buer Agarves, Ghanima is abducted and taken to Alia.

Most people now regard Leto as Shai-Hulud personified. Leto brings The Preacher and Halleck to Shuloch in a stolen ornithopter. There he subdues the Cast Out with a demonstration of his superhuman strength and commands them to gather and stockpile spice, to prepare an oasis for him that will serve as his home. Halleck still has many doubts about Leto and whether or not he is an Abomination. The Preacher tells him that Leto is a community, not a single being. He has been formed by crisis and survived a lethal environment: "He is the ultimate feedback system upon which our system depends. He'll reinsert into the system the results of its past performance" (375/373). Halleck finds The Preacher to be intensely alive, but he responds by saying that to be a god can ultimately become boring, even degrading. For his part Leto is torn by the old threads of his lost humanity, his life at times caught in primal anguish. He briefly contemplates walking away into the desert as his father had done, but realizes the trap of a partial commitment. Significantly, Leto no longer relies on pure vision but on vision management, and thinks of himself as a husbandman with mankind as his farm. While Tyekanik, Jessica, and Farad'n arrive on Arrakis, Leto takes The Preacher with him to Arrakeen to confront "the shattering crisis." At Arrakeen Alia awaits Farad'n. She prepares Ghanima as a Fremen bride equipped with a ceremonial knife in the hope that she will kill him. Like some latter-day John the Baptist, The Preacher denounces the sensuality and corruption of Alia in the plaza of her own temple. One of her overly zealous priests, outraged by what he takes to be blasphemy against her divine person, kills Paul with a knife. Before Alia can take any further action, however, Leto smashes his way into her chambers, takes Ghanima's arm and, uttering the words "Secher Nbiw," frees her from her self-induced compulsion. The months of self-hypnotic suppression have built for her a safe place and she has escaped Abomination, but madness now takes horrifying possession of Alia. After a brief struggle with Leto, in which many disconnected voices try to assert themselves—including the Baron Harkonnen—she commits suicide by leaping from a window to her death in the plaza below.

Everyone is now terrified of Leto who has become a kind of living god, everyone except Ghanima. She alone seems to understand the agony of his condition because he still retains the memory of what it means to be human. She tells Farad'n that Leto gives more than anyone ever gave before. Paul walked into the desert trying to escape possession by "the others," Alia became an Abomination in fear of them, and Jessica must use every Bene Gesserit wile to cope with the mere infancy of this condition. Only Ghanima is prepared to justify Leto's actions, including his taking over of the Bene Gesserit breeding program and his mating of Farad'n to Ghanima—though he marries her himself. Within a hundred years, she tells Farad'n, there will be fewer than fifty worms kept in a carefully managed reservation. Leto will control the spice absolutely in the lean years to come. But there will be a lasting peace until his Empire falls—in four thousand years—in Kralizec. And when that comes, humans will have renewed their memory of what it is like to be alive. All the worms will be dead within two hundred years, but the worms will return after Leto goes into the sand. His final metamorphosis will provide the seeds from which the universe will be reborn.

The final scene is one of Leto's investiture as God Emperor. Leto sits next to a jar containing the water of Muad'Dib. He gives Farad'n the position of Royal Scribe and renames him Harq al-Ada, which means

"Breaking of the Habit" (quotations from his writings open many sections of *Children of Dune*). He tells Stilgar that everything returns later in a changed form: "You have felt thoughts in your head; your descendants will feel thoughts in their bellies" (404/403). It is made clear that the pendulum will once more swing back again into its opposite: Leto's people will arise from their bellies great and beautiful and this time they will not forget the lesson he has taught them. Then he surprises Farad'n by telling him that there is always a "mystique"—religious, hero/leader, messiah, science/technology—in any civilization that leaves future generations unprepared for the universe's treachery. To overcome this tendency in his Empire he has himself committed two treacheries. First, although he has been telling everyone that he has escaped Abomination, in fact he has not. He is a community dominated by an ancient and surpassingly cruel and autocratic ancestor, Harum, about whom nothing else is said. Second, he will not marry Farad'n to his sister, but to himself, violating the Fremen taboo against incest. Leto will mold Farad'n's descendants in his own image, in the most intensive, the most inclusive training program in all of history: "We'll be an ecosystem in miniature" (408/406). Those descendants will survive Kralizec when Leto is gone, when the power of his spice monopoly fades, and when new powers appear throughout his realm. As *Children of Dune* closes, and with it the Dune trilogy, Leto vows to create a new consciousness in all men, but first humans must learn once more to live in their instincts.

Ecology, which to readers of *Dune* in the 1960s bore the promise that man might finally be able to understand and take responsibility for the consequences of his actions, is itself greatly transformed in *Children of Dune*. In the vision of Liet Kynes, the ecological transformation of Arrakis from desert into irrigated paradise was to have been a model of ecological foresight on a grand scale, and was to have taken approximately three hundred and fifty years. Indeed, Herbert conceived of Kynes himself as a model for what we popularly conceive of as the ecologically aware person who thinks of consequences. But Kynes is killed in *Dune* by the very planet he wished to transform, and by the time the events in *Children of Dune* unfold what started as ecological foresight has become a debacle of intrusive manipulation. Is Herbert then pessimistic about human ecology and mankind's attempts to adapt itself to its environment or, in other words, our ability to survive as a species? Herbert's thought is really too subtle to be called merely pessimistic. His intention in the Dune trilogy is revealed finally as an attempt to shatter the myth of Paul Atreides, to teach the reader a lesson in the dangers of hero worship. The prescience game turns out to be a trap which locks us into one future. Herbert, therefore, has Paul hand over his visions to his son Leto, who has different uses for them and a greater commitment to them over thousands of years. He does, however, choose one vision over the others, his "Golden Path," and we are bound to ask in what ways this future can be different from the others. Does not the Golden Path lock us into a single time line as well?

Not merely the Dune trilogy, but the meaning of the entire Dune series depends upon our interpretation of Leto's Golden Path. Of course, if we have learned anything about Herbert from reading the first three volumes, it is that there will be surprises along this path. Initially we think—and Herbert deliberately leads us to believe—that the Golden Path is Leto's three thousand years of enforced tyranny and stagnation. This prospect is truly appalling, and Leto seems willing to admit it, but it is the only way apparently to survive Kralizec and racial extinction. We are, I think, morally troubled by his decision, and may wonder where in the realm of values we are to situate ourselves. Is he really Satan? Only at the end of *God Emperor of Dune,* however, when Leto dies, do we learn that the Golden Path includes something else, a new kind of time without parallels, with no concurrent points on its curves.[3] All along Leto had been breeding descendants of the Atreides in a millennia-long experiment in human evolution that was to culminate in Siona Atreides, the first of the new Atreides line, capable of disappearing from prescient view. Siona and her descendants can never be tracked down by any Oracle. In her he creates the means of humanity's continued survival and his own destruction. In his last dialogues with Siona we come to understand something of the nature of his sacrifice (he gives up his chance to be human in order that mankind may survive) and the splendor of his gift. In other words we come to understand him, just as he had predicted. Leto's gift is infinity, and Herbert's efforts with Leto are an attempt to involve us in infinity as a paradox:

> The whole thrust of everything I've been doing in the Dune trilogy and again in the new book [*God Emperor of Dune*] is to point out a kind of paradox. In the first place I'm saying in there that paradox is a hand or a finger pointing at something else which is beyond it. If you encounter a paradox, that indicates something beyond it. The paradox should not be a barrier. It should be

an indicator, a waymarker. The paradox I'm addressing here is the paradox of infinity. Any finite defined time period—900 billion years—is a blip against infinity. You have to recognize this. And if you are talking about consequences to human survival, then you had better extend your time sense and leave it open-ended. That is the real definition of the Golden Path—the open-ended time sense. As long as the time sense is open then we are surviving. It has no linear direction, no choice of who is human. It just derives from human stock and goes on.[4]

When prompted to say more about the Golden Path by the interviewer, Herbert said only that with Leto "the Gate is open," and that more words would only make it less understandable. But it seems clear that a major shift in the understanding of prescience has been made in *Children of Dune.* The central paradox of the Dune trilogy concerns itself with the human vision of time and its relationship to prescience. In order for the Oracle to perform, Paul had to tangle himself in a web of predestination that negated all surprises. To desire absolute prediction is really to want today and to reject tomorrow and its freedoms. What Leto discovers in his visions is a way to *create* his Golden Path, not predict it. The overall design becomes manifest only in the last two volumes where Leto's many Dreaming Minds, now existing as "pearls of awareness" in the sandworms of Dune, are what hold the human-universe of reality on its course. This is what creates the reality he predicted. Not prediction, but creation. Nonetheless, the creative aspect of Leto's vision is apparent in *Children of Dune.* Throughout it all and by his own example, he says to us that he creates his Golden Path by risking his life and by daring to confront an infinite universe. Now it is up to us. For his part Herbert creates a sense of infinity in the reader through his use of loopholes in dialogues and recurrent themes that turn back upon themselves paradoxically. Indeed, paradox is a figure of speech much appreciated by Leto—an absolute ruler who does not believe in absolutes—as we will see in the next chapter.

Chapter Five

God Emperor of Dune

The events in *God Emperor of Dune* take place more than thirty-five hundred years after Leto's ascension to the throne. Leto's Golden Path continues, as does his enforced Peace which is based on an economy simplified in the extreme: no interest charges permitted, cash on the barrelhead. The only coinage bears a likeness of Leto's cowled face. Yet the economy is based, totally, on melange, a natural substance no longer produced on Dune or anywhere else in Leto's multigalactic Empire, a substance whose value, already enormous, keeps increasing. Without melange to ignite the linear prescience of Guild Navigators, people cross the parsecs of space only at a snail's crawl. Without melange, the Bene Gesserit cannot endow Truthsayers or Reverend Mothers. Without the geriatric properties of melange, people live and die according to the ancient measure—no more than a hundred years or so. Now, melange is held only in Guild and Bene Gesserit storehouses, with a few small hoards among the remnants of the Great Houses, and Leto's gigantic hoard which they all covet. They would like to raid him, but do not dare, fearing he would destroy it before surrendering it. Instead they come hat in hand to petition Leto for melange. He doles it out as a reward and holds it back as a punishment. By this means Leto enforces tranquillity. All of the sandworms are gone. Leto is the last link with the sandworms, which had produced the original stockpiles of melange, and if he dies away from water, there will be no more spice—not ever.

Leto keeps a Citadel in the middle of his Sareer—a replica-in-miniature of the planetary desert that once covered the surface of Arrakis. The Sareer is his way of ensuring that some part of the old Fremen ways are preserved other than in museums. Leto uses the desert as a testing ground for some of the descendants of the Atreides, and much of the action of *God Emperor* takes place in the Sareer or in the Citadel. Because of its artificially maintained dryness, the Sareer is also the only place on Arrakis where he can feel comfortable in the last stages of his metamorphosis from human to sandworm. Leto has virtually become one body with the sandtrout skin he put on so many centuries ago and has entered into the pre-worm stage. His body is seven meters long and somewhat more than two meters in diameter, ribbed for most of its length. His legs and feet have mostly atrophied, but his hands and arms are still recognizable as human, as is his Atreides face which peers out from beneath a cowl of skin. The whole of this gross body weighs nearly five tons.

Leto carries his weight around mostly on his Royal Cart, a mechanism of Ixian manufacture. The Ixians are important in this volume as a source of forbidden technology (they are experimenting with machines that have the potential to replace Guild Navigators who can operate only on melange). Although he has forbidden the training of mentats, Leto has ceased to enforce so strictly the millennia-long ban against thinking machines and even has begun to use certain Ixian products himself that would have been anathema in his early reign. In addition to his Royal Cart, there is also the "no-room" (which emits no detectable radiation) where Leto keeps his archives, including his personal journals. The journals themselves are printed by an Ixian device known as a dictatel in the no-room. If Leto casts his thoughts in a particular mode, the dictatel is activated and the words are printed on "ridulian crystal sheets" only one molecule thick.

Leto's archives, known as the "Rakis Finds" by archaeologists, are not uncovered until nearly two thousand years after his death. In fact, *God Emperor* opens with an excerpt from a speech made by Hadi Benotto, a Bene Gesserit, announcing with obvious excitement the discoveries at Dar-es-Balat on Rakis (incidentally, Benotto is also the imaginary editor of *The Dune Encyclopedia*). The historical epoch known as "The Scattering" has already occurred and the remnants of Leto's Empire are beginning to return to Dune. A section from Hadi Benotto's translation of Leto's journals is included as a later chapter. In it Leto says that his purpose was to be the greatest predator ever known. His tone in this excerpt, which evidently marks the opening of his journals, is that of one amused at the temporal paradox of finding a beginning: Leto writes with a foreknowledge that he will one day be a sandworm of enormous size and potency, a foreknowledge registered in the journals in anticipation of an event that his audience will know as something long past or indeed almost mythical. He writes primarily to personalize himself to readers of the far future, for he anticipates that he will be misunderstood as an inhuman monster devoid of feelings.

Sometimes, however, Leto orders copies of his journals printed on material of lesser permanence. It is two of these latter types that are stolen by Siona Atreides in a raid on his Citadel, which provides the opening action of the book. The raid is undertaken, however, not to steal the journals, but to find the plans of Leto's Citadel so that his spice hoard can then be located. Their theft by Siona, daughter of Moneo Atreides, the majordomo and chief aide to Leto—himself a former rebel now converted to the Golden Path—is a daring exploit. But she and her companions pay a high price for them and for the Citadel plans. Of ten rebels, only Siona survives. The others are brought down by Leto's patrolling D-wolves before they can reach the Idaho River. The rebels believed that they found the books by chance, but since Leto is known to have feared that his actions would be misunderstood in times to come unless he arranged for revelations to be made, the convenient placement of two of his journals next to the Citadel plans may not, it is strongly suggested, have been an accident. At any rate, within a few weeks of the Citadel raid, Siona arranges for copies of the stolen books to be sent to the Bene Gesserit, the Ixians, and the Spacing Guild. This last group finally breaks Leto's cipher and translates them. Selections from *The Stolen Journals* open almost every section of *The God Emperor,* injecting a first-person context into the narrative.

Leto thinks that the elaborate series of catacombs beneath his Citadel are the most interesting place in the universe because they contain the water, the bones, the dust of his ancestors and of the Atreides who have lived and died since the Dune times (they represent the results of his breeding program) as well as the remains of the Duncans. Here he interviews the latest Duncan Idaho ghola—there have been many over the centuries supplied by the Tleilaxu, but unlike Hayt they come with their original memories and without metal eyes—who is going to attempt to kill him. Ostensibly Idaho, as the Captain of Leto's Palace Guards (all women) comes to report on Siona's raid, but he is secretly in league with the rebels because he feels that the Imperium has wandered too far from the old Atreides morality and has, in fact, become a juggernaut that crushes the innocent in its path. He hides an Ixian lasgun in his briefcase, hoping to get a clear shot at Leto's face, which seems to him a kind of obscenity, a lost bit of humanity trapped in something alien. It is evident that Leto has played out this scenario many times before with other Duncans. For the most part he is bored during the interview and drifts off into memories of other conversations with the other Duncans, even though he knows about the lasgun. This momentary introspection provides the Duncan with an opportunity to fire, but Leto startles him by using the angry Voice of his father, Paul Muad'Dib, and, rolling from his cart, crushes the Duncan to death with only minor damage to himself. Leto loves surprises in his Duncans, even nasty ones, but this Duncan has been all too predictable. Like all of the others he had wanted to know how many of him there had been before and how they had been disposed of. Although Leto desires the Duncans as his constant companions through the centuries, hoping to find surprises, the Duncans always seem to end by asking in derision how many times they must pay the debt of loyalty.

In Onn, Leto's Festival City and the major population center on Arrakis, Leto has a spy among the conspirators. Nayla is Herbert's model of the worshipful servant and fanatic. She will do anything for her Lord Leto, even obey Siona in all things, as Leto has commanded her to do. By means of another Ixian device, a computer, which fills her with unease, she communicates the plans of the rebels to Leto. But Siona trusts Nayla entirely because of her devoted nature.

Leto does not need Nayla to tell him that Siona is his ardent enemy, however. He has been observing Siona for some time, and knows that she is a woman of action who lives on the surface of enormous energies, energies that fill him with fantasies of delight. He cannot contemplate those living energies without a feeling of ecstasy. They are his reason for being, the justification of everything he has done. For Siona is the *new*; he is a collection of the obsolete, a mere crypt of his ancestors who occasionally rise up in a chorus of protests against him. Leto's Golden Path remains, to be sure, but surprisingly Siona can fade from prescient view at times. She is a unique phenomenon, not prescient herself, but seemingly embodying all those traits of survival Leto has wanted to breed into the human race. Soon, however, she must be tested by Leto.

Leto discusses "the delicate nature of Siona's present fortunes" with her father, Moneo. Siona is Moneo's only child and naturally he pleads for her safety, but the God Emperor has bred her to be dangerous and unpredictable. To him Siona is like a clean slate upon which great things may yet be written. Siona is the contrast by which he knows his deepest fears about the sameness and boredom that could break the Golden Path. This sameness extends to both the nature of authority and rebellion against authority, a pattern that Leto has seen repeated countless times, a pattern that, it is implied, will always end in reconstituting "the pharaonic disease." Leto hopes that he will be the last of a long line of such rulers: "We are the myth-killers, you and I, Moneo. That's the dream we share. I assure you from a God's Olympian perch that government is a shared myth. When the myth dies, the government dies."[1] The debate about authority, power, rebellion, and their relationship to technology (recall that Duncan has tried to kill Leto with an Ixian lasgun, a forbidden device) extends to the "inner arena" of Leto's ancestral memories. Indeed, there seems to be as much dialogue with these voices as there is with external characters, making *God Emperor of Dune* the most overtly dialogical novel in the Dune series although Leto does not allow these other voices (external or internal) to have much independence. Yet it is clear that he despises his own seemingly absolute position in these dialogues, calling it elsewhere "the ultimate rhetorical despotism" (89/85). Leto concludes the debate with his inner voices by proclaiming that technology breeds anarchy because it puts terrible weapons in the hands of the individual. He goes off to his tower to mourn the death of his latest Duncan as Moneo informs him that the new Duncan is already on his way from the Tleilaxu.

The next scene opens with the arrival of the new Duncan who reflects on his ghola nature and on what the "dirty Tleilaxu" may have done to him in the way of conditioning. He is interrogated by women of Leto's Imperial Guard and is addressed as "Commander Idaho." As might be expected, Duncan wants to know how many there have been before him, and throughout the scene he tries to ascertain whether the stories the Tleilaxu have told him about the intervening millennia are true or not. The Tleilaxu histories had not mentioned the absence of mentats—surely the Atreides must still have a need for them, he thinks. Duncan does not like the sound of fanaticism that he hears in the voices of the Guards (who are also Fish Speakers), yet feels secure in the integrity of the Atreides.

Meanwhile, in a service room beneath the Festival City of Onn, the rebels hold a meeting which revives certain forbidden Fremen ceremonies, including the use of a plastic replica of a crysknife (Nayla is the only rebel who owns a real one, given to her by the God Emperor), a contraband copy bought from the Museum Fremen. Iyo Kobat, the Ambassador from Ix who is about to be expelled for his role in the plot against Leto, visits the rebels. He tells them of Ixian plans to make a machine that will replace the Guild Navigators and their dependence on spice. The God Emperor, or Worm, as he is called by the rebels, has told them they that may continue developing the device as long as they provide him with daily reports on their progress. Kobat is to take this message back to the Ixians. Siona scoffs at Kobat, telling him that the "real" message is that Worm knows the device is a lie and a cheat, that it will never work, and that the Ixians have involved the Guild and the Bene Gesserit only to get their supplies of melange. The Worm's real message to the Ixians is to continue cheating because it amuses him. Kobat angrily reminds Siona of the fate of other rebels who have challenged the Worm's authority, including her own father Moneo: he gives them a little rope with which to play at rebellion and then hauls them in as recruits to his inner circle. Before leaving, Kobat reveals that Leto has asked for an extension to his cart, for more ridulian crystal sheets, and that the Ixian's next ambassador will be the niece of Malky, once an ambassador himself, Hwi Noree. Siona dismisses Korbat, sending him off with copies of the journals stolen from Leto's Citadel, while knowing that this is precisely what the Worm wants her to do.

There follows an excerpt from the official job interview Noree has with the Inquisitors of Ix. Noree, like her uncle Malky, admires Leto as the most supremely artful diplomat in the Empire, as "a master conversationalist," who is expert in any subject. She also perceives a certain Atreides nobility in Leto's actions, believing that he made the desperate choice of becoming a sandworm not for longevity or power, but because he saw something in their future that only such a sacrifice would prevent. Despite her apparent sympathies for the God Emperor, and against our expectations, Hwi Noree is confirmed as ambassador to the Court of Lord Leto.

In Leto's Citadel Moneo, looking tired, is busy attending to all of the upcoming business: Leto's decennial peregrination to Onn is at hand with all of its tiresome business of off-planet visitors vying with one another for more melange, the ritual with the Fish Speakers (Leto's private woman army), the new ambassadors, the changing of the Imperial Guard, the retirements and appointments, and a new Duncan Idaho to fit into the smooth workings of the imperial apparatus. What is more, Moneo realizes that it is Leto's intention to breed Siona with the new Duncan because he gives Leto access to a first-generation cross between an older human form and current products of his breeding program. But Moneo finds it peculiar to think of the Duncan as both an ancestor and as the father of his descendants. In seeking to understand the laws of Leto's breeding program and what he hopes to achieve by them, Moneo prompts Leto to reveal the key word: *predator.* Like a predator, Leto is improving the stock of humanity. Leto longs for a humankind that can make truly long-term decisions, and the key to that ability is an understanding of infinity. He tells Moneo that time runs out for any finite observer, that there are no closed systems, and that even he only stretches the finite matrix: "Moneo, even my thousands of years are but a puny blip against Infinity" (73/66). Leto sympathizes with Moneo's concern for Siona whom he must now test, but he knows that all of humankind is *his* only child.

There follows an assessment of the state of the Empire in the year 3508 of the reign of the Lord Leto, written by the Bene Gesserit. It seems that a certain Sister Chenoeh was invited to accompany the Fish Speakers in an entourage that accompanied one of Lord Leto's infrequent peregrinations, and her conversations with him are the most important aspect of the report. Leto knows that the Bene Gesserit has tried, without success, to suborn his Fish Speakers (his houris as Malky used to call them), but he says he will not harm Sister Chenoeh because of this. Instead, he will use her to send a message to the Bene Gesserit. In effect, he says that he has not destroyed them yet because they are so close, and yet so far, from his own designs. He wants to restore "outward spiritual freedom," the outward view, to mankind. However, the Bene Gesserit of all people should know the dangers of breeding for a particular characteristic, of seeking a defined genetic goal. In seeking the Kwisatz Haderach, they eventually got Leto, the wild card, and he in turn has achieved Siona.

Back at Leto's Citadel, Nayla visits the God Emperor to affirm her faith in his Godhead. As one of his most fanatical Fish Speakers, Nayla will do anything he asks, and Leto once again commands her to obey Siona in everything, even if Siona requires her to kill him. The irony of their conversations is that no matter what Leto says, even to the point of saying that the religion built around his person is a "holy obscenity" that disgusts him, and that it should end with him, Nayla's faith is so nearly absolute that she believes that her God is simply testing her in different ways. When he tells her that religions create radicals and fanatics like her, she solemnly thanks him.

After his interview with Nayla, Leto descends to his crypt in the late evening to meet the new Duncan. He purposefully leaves the interview chamber dark so that the Duncan will not be overcome by the sight of him. He also brings Paul Muad'Dib's voice into play in order to reassure the Duncan. In order to win his confidence, Leto reveals some secrets about himself that the Duncan will have to guard: that he is not a god and is vulnerable (especially to love, though he does not tell the Duncan this directly), and that the sandworm body he inhabits—which he dramatically reveals to him in bright light—will one day produce new sandworms that will be different: they will have more neural ganglia and consequently will be aware. The Duncan seems most concerned, however, about the nature of Leto's female army, the Fish Speakers, which he is to command. In the next scene, set the following morning, he asks Moneo about Leto's purposes in creating such an army, after experiencing a terrifying nightmare in which he sees weaponless women in black armor rushing for him, waving hands moist with red blood, their mouths open to display terrible fangs. Moneo explains that Leto believes that an all-female army is more protective of life and survival and will not turn against the civilian populace once the external threat has been disposed of. Leto believes that the male army, once it breaks out of its adolescent and homosexual restraints, is essentially rapist. Idaho at first reacts to all of this angrily, but because he prides himself on self-honesty, he recalls incidents in his own experience where sadomasochistic cults of youth had been preserved in the military.

Four days later Leto begins his peregrination to Onn, his Festival City. As he drives his Royal Cart, Moneo walks beside him and they discuss Siona and Duncan Idaho, who follows the procession at the head of the Fish Speakers. It is obvious to Leto that his new Guard Commander does not enjoy the presence of the courtiers of whom he is very suspicious. Leto likes the alertness of the new Duncan, though he forbids him to march out in front where he could be most effective in an attack. He wants Moneo to introduce Siona to the Duncan immediately. Moneo is anxious for his daughter, whom he considers foolish, but is equally wary of the growing Worm signs in Leto—the look of brooding which comes over his face when his eyes close or glaze over—signs which can explode in wild violence. Leto's symbiosis with the sandtrout remains a mystery to Moneo. If accounts are to be believed, the sandtrout skin makes his body almost invulnerable to both time and violence. The great ecological cycle that had produced melange lies within the God Emperor, marking time. Moneo realizes that it was his fascination with this unpredictable creature, who never ceases to surprise and amaze him, that finally brought him to heel. He is well aware, however, that the Worm could easily murder him in a fit of violence.

Ahead in Onn, two Bene Gesserit sisters, Anteac and Luyseyal, are disturbed to learn that their audience with the God Emperor has been moved to the last position because all of the spice allotments will be fixed or even gone by that time. Anteac is, in fact, a Mentat, the training of whom has been outlawed by Leto. She uses her abilities to calculate the odds that Leto has found out about their plot, undertaken with the Ixians and the Tleilaxu, against him. The plans have gone awry and have been taken over by the Tleilaxu who have replaced nearly everyone with their Face Dancer substitutes. They intend to attack Leto on the road to Onn. Considering Leto's prescient powers, the Sisters consider this attack to be the ultimate folly and thus make haste to distance themselves from the Tleilaxu by warning Leto of the plot.

Meanwhile, on the road to Onn, Leto and Moneo continue their discussion. Leto rails against the Bene Gesserit and all religions, which in his view employ rhetorical despotism to make people into willing servants: "Before the Bene Gesserit, the Jesuits were the best at it" (122/117). Moneo realizes that the Reverend Mothers are in for a bad time, as is House Corrino which has attempted to bribe him. Leto orders the Corrino killed, remarking in passing that while it is still known that melange can extend human life, the spice can shorten life as well. The topics of melange and human time make Moneo recall his first glimpse of Leto's hidden hoard, glowing radiant blue in the dim silver light of arabesqued glowglobes. Only the God Emperor knows where the hoard is hidden, and time has a different meaning for him than for Moneo (though Leto insists that Moneo can grasp the meaning of infinite time from him, but he will not). Leto tells Moneo that someday he will return to the sand and be the source of the spice. In addition, he will produce something just as wonderful (more sand-trout), a hybrid and prolific breeder. Within three hundred years a new kind of sandworm will reign on Dune. It will have animal awareness and a new cunning. The spice will be more dangerous to seek and far more perilous to keep as Shai-Hulud rises once more from the deeps. Leto reminds himself that Moneo is also his creation, and cannot be blamed for his fear and lack of understanding. In fact, the general tenor of their dialogues is signaled by Moneo's name, which is a Latin verb, connected with the word *mens* or *mind,* denoting to remind, admonish, or warn. What is more, the neuter plural of the participle of this verb, *monita,* was used in Vergil and other Classical Latin authors to mean *prophecies.* Considering Herbert's early education at the hands of Jesuits, it seems likely that this choice of a name for his majordomo accomplishes a deliberate irony. By the way, Bene Gesserit means "that it may be borne or accomplished well," and is derived from the hortative subjunctive of the Latin verb *gero,* meaning "to bear or carry away" in its root sense, but also "to conduct oneself in society."

The account of the Bene Gesserit Sister Chenoeh's dialogue with the God Emperor, found among her papers after her death, follows next in the narrative. Leto tells Sister Chenoeh that he will speak to her as if she were a page in one of his journals. After admonishing her about the many traps that language presents to the understanding, especially its inability to carry the truth without ambiguity, he tells her that "the greatest mystery of all time" and mystery by which he composes his life, is that "The only past which endures lies wordlessly within you" (134/129). Language conceals the truth as much as reveals it, and to put the truth into language is to risk being misunderstood, and to be subject to the erosion of meaning through historical time. Thus Leto knows that those who will one day read his journals in search of *the* truth about him will inevitably misunderstand: "The harder you try the more remote I will become until I vanish into eternal myth—a Living God at last!" (133/128). Leto tells Sister Chenoeh that the wordless movement of terrible events lies just below the surface of his journals. She is indeed terrified by his portentous words, but nonetheless feels she knows what he means by the wordless truth.

It seems that Herbert is deliberately slowing down the pace of the action in this book in order to textualize discourse—to make us aware of how and why texts are produced, to make us confront the fact of textuality as something apart from the mere representation of speech. The irony seems to be that texts, or at least historical texts, are produced by the human desire to locate and pronounce *the* truth about some event. Yet texts inevitably and scandalously proliferate in the human desire also to have the last word about some event, to supplant what others have said. Leto himself is trying to have the last word in the very act of writing his journals and in postponing their historical appearance. Chenoeh, in another of Leto's temporal paradoxes, is instructed on pain of death for the Bene Gesserit order to keep his words secret for a while. To make his point about textual truth being subject to the historical misappropriation of others even more ironic, Herbert ends this section with an archivist's note to the effect that the discovery of this private record is now little more than a footnote to history because of intervening events. The note also points out further texts in the Archive Records which anyone interested in the account may pursue—no doubt, it is implied, with the goal in mind of producing their own text, as Willis McNelly did with his *Dune Encyclopedia.*

Back on the Royal Road to Onn a group of Museum Fremen, degenerate relics of the once-proud desert warriors, begin to petition Leto. As they approach, Moneo sees the flesh of the approaching faces melt away in Face Dancer mockery, every face resolving into a likeness of Duncan Idaho. Imperial Guards and Face Dancers collide in a battle of lasguns and disorienting white noise produced by Leto's Royal Cart which flies off into the air. A thick knot of Fish Speakers forms around Duncan Idaho to protect him. Duncan takes off his clothes and runs naked so that he can be identified among the false Duncans. This action amuses and surprises Leto, moving him to laughter. The Duncan has become in effect a Greek warrior-messenger dashing to report the outcome to his commander. The condensation of history stuns Leto's memories, but Idaho is angry because the Fish Speakers would not let him fight. More than thirty of Leto's people and fifty Face Dancers are killed in the engagement. Except for some lasgun damage to the canopy of his Royal Cart, Leto is unharmed. He decides to have the Tleilaxu Ambassador publicly flogged and expelled but otherwise makes no public acknowledgment that the battle has even occurred.

By midafternoon the Royal Entourage comes down the final slope into the precincts of the Festival City. Throngs line the streets to greet them, and Leto's Fish Speakers begin to chant the words of the ritual called Siaynoq—the Feast of Leto, in which only females are allowed to participate. Moneo, of course, has been instructed in the ritual meanings of the word *Siaynoq,* but to him it means mystery, prestige, and power, and it invokes a license to act in the name of God. Although he claims that he *is* this ritual, Leto sometimes shares Siaynoq with a Duncan. This Duncan, however, seems more concerned with the possible means of defending Leto from attack in a city such as Onn, which is built around a central plaza where Leto can display himself to a worshipful populace.

During the private audience period preceding the festival proper, Leto interviews the new Ixian Ambassador, Hwi Noree, and quickly becomes fascinated and delighted with the basic sweetness of her nature, despite the devious training she has obviously had at the hands of the Bene Gesserit and the Ixians. She seems timeless to him—outside of time in a deeply peaceful way. Out of his thronging ancestral memories, Leto can see her as an idealized nun, kindly and self-sacrificing, all sincerity. There is no mistaking the deep sadness in her for the humanity Leto has sacrificed. She appears the epitome of goodness, obviously bred and conditioned for this quality by her Ixian masters with their careful calculations of the effect this would have on the

God Emperor. Hwi Noree is not openly seductive, yet this very fact makes her profoundly seductive to Leto. In another life they would have been friends, even lovers, companions in an ultimate sharing between the sexes. Hwi Noree's masters had planned for her to know this as well. Leto then reflects on how cruel these "criminals of science" are to send her, knowing what her pain will be. He reviews his reasons for tolerating the Ixians, which include the fact that they operate in the terra incognita of creative invention outlawed by the Butlerian Jihad. They make their devices, such as Leto's dictatel machine, in the image of the mind. He vows to make Hwi Noree the permanent Ixian Ambassador.

He apparently tolerates the Tleilaxu for another reason. They still have the cells of the original Duncan Idaho and can supply Leto with another Duncan whenever he wishes. This does not stop him, however, from threatening to send the current Duncan off to destroy the Tleilaxu home world in his interview with the Tleilaxu Ambassador, Duro Nunepi. Leto reveals nothing about the Face Dancer attack on the Royal Road, but instead claims he is angry because of lies being spread by the Tleilaxu about his "disgusting sexual habits." Nunepi is stunned. The accusation is a bold lie itself, completely unexpected. He can only gape as Leto tells him that the spice allotment will pass over the Tleilaxu for the next decade, and that he is going to be publicly flogged. Idaho objects that nothing good can come of this action but Leto responds by saying that is precisely what he wants.

Leto's interview with the Bene Gesserit delegation that same evening also reveals why he tolerates them in his Empire. Both Anteac and Luyseyal are Truthsayers: they can tell when false accounts are being given. Anteac is much older than Luyseyal, but the latter is reputed to be the best Truthsayer the Bene Gesserit have. They are also both Reverend Mothers, and of all people in his Empire Reverend Mothers are most like him—but limited to the memories of only their female ancestors and the collateral female identities of their inheritance ritual. Still, each of them does exist as somewhat of an integrated mob. In this interview they have won some small favor in Leto's eyes because they warned him, albeit belatedly, about the Face Dancer attack. Nonetheless, it amuses Leto to greet such delegations in the voice and persona of Jessica, his Bene Gesserit grandmother, and to display controlled feminine tones with just a hint of mockery. Through their dialogues with the God Emperor, they are constantly seeking to find out more about his strange metamorphosis and to discover any chink in his armor. This time they have relied on the Oral History and Bene Gesserit records that say that concentrated spice-essence shatters the worm, precipitating its dissolution. They have brought a small vial of this priceless substance, and Luyseyal tries to get close enough to throw it at Leto. Leto smells it almost immediately, however, and the plot fails when he hints to them through indirect, hidden messages in his speech that he knows about it. Leto mocks them and their supposed Truthsaying abilities, but tells them he will continue their present spice allotment over the next decade.

That night of the first Audience Day, as Fish Speakers fight small skirmishes with Face Dancers in the city, thoughts of madness assail Leto. The Ixians have found out his secret—that he still desires his humanity. He is so in love with Hwi that he desperately searches for ways that might reverse the terrible metamorphosis he is undergoing. But there are none. He thinks wildly of abandoning the Golden Path, but the many voices within him remind him of the oath he has taken with them that allowed him to preserve his sanity. The only antidote to his agony is to lose himself for a time in his own past, striking backward along the axis of memories. He toys with the idea of taking a tour through sexual dalliances and exploits, but realizes that he cannot make that choice, not this night, not with Hwi Noree out there in his city. He then realizes how useless his past is now that he has encountered Hwi, and that the special dream-state that he creates throughout his Empire has produced something new. He is a hunter caught in his own net. Leto weeps silently.

The next morning Idaho and Siona are sent out of the city by Imperial ornithopter to be taken to a safe place. They are to return the following morning for the ritual of Siaynoq, though Siona will be sent to the Citadel. Leto intends to breed Siona and Duncan, although Duncan is much more impressed with Hwi Noree whom he has met only briefly. Siona is hostile to any of the Worm's plans for her. In order to completely alienate Duncan she has the ornithopter stop at the village of Goygoa, the former Shuloch, where an unsuspecting Duncan meets the children and wife of the previous Duncan. This meeting is one of the most dramatic in the book. He is shocked to find that the woman, named Irti, has a face out of his deepest fantasies: she looks exactly like Jessica, Muad'Dib's mother recreated in new flesh. After seeing how painfully human the ghola's reactions are, especially toward his young son, Siona is sorry, and she and Duncan end this episode as rather uneasy friends.

On the following morning in Onn, Duncan leads Leto on his Royal Cart in the Feast of Siaynoq. In effect, Leto tempts Duncan with a share in almost absolute power, for the Fish Speakers worship him as well as Leto. Duncan, true to his nature, wants to know *why* Leto has created an all-female army with which to enforce tranquillity, Leto's Peace. In answering him, Leto delivers what amounts to a devastating feminist critique of male power roles (he does have all of the female memories of his ancestors), telling Duncan that with his female army he prepares a way for the entire species to overcome adolescence by having men learn survival at the hands of women instead of the other way around. The ceremony itself involves the eating and sharing of a melange-impregnated wafer and the displaying, by Leto, of Paul Muad'Dib's crysknife. Made from the tooth of a giant sandworm, it reminds everyone that the return of Shai-Hulud depends upon Leto. What Leto is working toward is a binding sense of mutual dependence throughout the Empire. When Duncan says he does not feel bound to the Fish Speakers, Leto reminds him that such things take time and that Duncan is the ancient norm against which the new can be measured. Slowly, Duncan feels the restrained passion in the touches of the Fish Speakers as they march out of the ceremony and knows the deepest fear in his experience.

In the late evening of the Festival's third day Leto summons Hwi Noree to his audience chamber and tells her more of his past and his future. Leto's godhead began among the Fremen when he told them it was no longer possible for him to give his death-water to the tribe. Leto told the Fremen that his water would be consecrated to a Supreme Deity, and later became that deity to them by using his many different voices. Hwi finds these actions manipulative, but Leto asks her not to judge him harshly. He then tells her of the awful fragmentation he will face—a horror that his father tried to prevent—when the sandtrout return to the sand. During this process, which he characterizes as "the infinite division and subdivision of a blind identity," he will nonetheless be still aware, but mute: "A little pearl of awareness will go with every sandworm and every sandtrout—knowing yet unable to move a single cell, aware in an endless dream" (219/219). Hwi Noree shudders at such revelations, eyes widening with shock when he tells her that she will be his bride. After Noree leaves, Leto calls in his Duncan and tells him to stay away from her.

On the morning of the fourth Festival day Moneo enters Leto's chamber early to tell him that Anteac is a mentat, a fact that Leto already knows. He permits this form of disobedience because it amuses him. Leto instructs Moneo to allow Siona to read the copies of his translated stolen journals that will be arriving that day from the Guild. Moneo reports what he knows about the origins of Hwi Noree—that Malky, the former Ixian Ambassador, was involved in a "cellular restructuring" (a Tleilaxu term) that produced her. Indeed, Hwi Noree is the mirror of the redoubtable Malky, his opposite in everything, including sex. Moneo fears the effect of melange on Siona and that there might be some hidden in the package from the Guild, but Leto reassures him. There follows a long dialogue on the effects of melange on those possessing Atreides genes. For some of them it may "roll the mystery of Time through a peculiar process of internal revelation" (232/232). Moneo refuses fearfully to take melange, although it would lengthen his life. Leto orders Moneo to bring him Hwi Noree.

Less than an hour later Moneo brings Hwi. Leto tells her of the dangers of the Ixians.[2] They once contemplated making a weapon—a type of hunter-seeker, self-propelled death with a machine mind. It was designed as a self-improving thing that would seek out life and reduce it to inorganic matter. The Ixians do not recognize that machine-makers always run the risk of turning themselves into machines. In Leto's view this is the ultimate sterility. He points out that machines always fail, given time. When the machines fail, nothing will be left, no life at all. We may infer, and it seems certain from dialogues later in the novel (342/348) where Leto is sensitizing Siona to the demands of the Golden Path, that this is the terrible path of racial extinction Leto has forseen in his visions. The Golden Path, which Leto defines as "the eternal thread of all humankind by whatever definition" (339/345), prevents this apocalypse because it will produce humans, the descendants of Siona, who cannot be tracked by predatory machines. Before that terrible time in which humans will be hunted, and before the sandworm reigns once more on Arrakis, Leto knows that he will die four deaths: the death of the flesh, the death of the soul, the death of the myth, and the death of reason. All of these deaths contain also the seed of his resurrection. However, Leto does not elaborate on this concept, preferring to speak, as usual, in oracular paradoxes. He admits to Hwi, however, that his Golden Path does allow for the possibility of failure.

That night, as darkness enfolds the city of Onn, a shattering explosion, set off by the rebels and the Tleilaxu, rocks the Ixian Embassy. Furious because of the threat to his beloved Hwi, Leto enters the fray, his flailing body slipping and slithering in the blood from his crushed enemies. Blood is buffered water to him, but nonetheless the water ignites blue smoke from every flexion where it slips through the sandtrout skin. This fills him with water-agony that in turn ignites more violence. Leto, exhausted, goes to a secret room where blasts of superheated dry air cleanse and restore him. As he emerges from the cleansing room he learns that Hwi, although slightly wounded, is safe and will be brought to him as soon as the local commander thinks it prudent. Although there are no survivors of the attack, Leto deduces that Malky is the perpetrator and arranges to have him brought to Arrakis for execution. Leto is glad that his gentle Hwi has not seen him in action as the violent Worm. He knows that he could have been killed in the attack, but merely tells her that he is being tested.

The following morning Leto has some Face Dancers that were captured earlier perform an ancient Fremen wedding dance for him and Hwi. The Fish Speakers cheer loudly, but are nonetheless disturbed because Leto had said they were his only brides in the ritual of Siaynoq. Leto tells Moneo that they will return to the Citadel that evening, but Moneo is furious at the idea of Leto's marriage, arguing that disgusting rumors of Leto's sexuality will spread throughout the Empire. Leto is unperturbed, saying that the defiling of the god is an ancient human tradition. He is delighted that strong human emotions have returned to him again. Leto instructs Moneo that he wishes to wed Hwi Noree in Sietch Tabr Village, but leaves the date up to Moneo. At any rate it will not occur before Leto has tested Siona. In thinking about Moneo's responses, Leto judges that Moneo has locked himself into his past. In another interview following soon after this one Duncan Idaho also is obsessed with his past reincarnations. He accuses the God Emperor of having committed the crime of taking all of the magic out of his life. Because he remembers dying, life never truly begins again for him, but is overshadowed by the past. Duncan stalks off angrily when he learns that the God Emperor truly intends to marry Hwi Noree. Leto reflects how like a little boy Duncan is—the oldest man in the universe and the youngest, both in one flesh.

On the third full day back from the decennial Festival in Onn, Leto is himself coldly angry because the Duncan has been disobeying him in seeing Hwi Noree. Moneo is truly terrified that the Worm will kill him. He tries to reassure his Lord that Hwi has nothing but sympathy for him because he is a ghola with no roots in their time. Yet Leto knows that the Duncans have always been exceedingly attractive to women. Leto is seemingly caught in a painful bind: the Duncan is not for Hwi, yet he cannot bring himself to hurt her in any way. Trembling with fright, Moneo leaves Leto's aerie. As he descends, he can hear the God Emperor thumping his heavy body against the stones of his chamber.

With patient care, Leto prepares his first private meeting with Siona since her childhood banishment to the Fish Speaker schools in the Festival City. He will see her at the Little Citadel, a vantage tower he has built in the central Sareer. He spends part of the day luxuriously crawling through the sands, the natural element of his worm nature. Shortly after noon, his worm-self satiated, Leto enters his tower and spends the rest of the day thinking and plotting. Just about nightfall Moneo brings Siona. Leto tells her that he needs to find out what Time has done to her and tries to win her sympathy by revealing how much he has suffered on the Golden Path, how much he hungers for his lost humanity. Although he clearly detects the beginnings of a reluctant sympathy in Siona because of these revelations—after all, they are both Atreides, and Leto was a child when he took on such responsibilities—she still sneers at him and his sacrifices because she thinks him a despot, responsible only to himself. Leto discovers through further questioning about how she views the future that Siona does not trust her instincts, her untrained abilities at prediction. He sends her back to the Citadel, warning her that the next time they meet they will learn what she is made of.

At the Citadel Moneo tries to warn Duncan again not to see Hwi Noree, but he goes off defiantly, finds Noree willing and waiting in his chambers, and makes love to her. All along Duncan has refused to be the God Emperor's stud, and his lovemaking with Noree is an act of defiance in which he risks his life. Noree, however, fully intends to wed Leto because she loves him. She does not believe that Leto will destroy them. A while later Leto summons Moneo to the darkness of his crypt. It seems obvious that he knows about Duncan and Hwi, for although he gives Moneo a long angry lecture about the master-servant relationship that all religions create, he ends by telling Moneo that he intended Hwi Noree to mate with him. As Moneo leaves, dumbfounded, Leto exclaims that he will test Siona tomorrow. As the sun rises over the desert, Siona walks behind Leto who glides over the dunes of his Sareer. She has read Leto's journals, has heard the admonitions of her father (especially about how to use the stillsuit she now wears), but is not sure what to think or to expect as a test. As they progress through Leto's artificially controlled desert—maintained by Ixian weather satellites—she climbs up on his back at his invitation, and they discuss the customs of their common Fremen ancestors. Leto keeps pointing out the Infinity of the desert, stretching flatly from horizon to horizon, and the fact that they leave no tracks behind them in the sand. He thus makes Siona feel her past and tries to sensitize her to her future on the Golden Path. Siona, however, does not want to be part of the Golden Path. She foolishly does not pull the face flap of her stillsuit across her mouth so that the suit can recycle her moisture. She wants her mouth free for talking. Leto does not warn her of the danger of dehydration.

Back at the Citadel Moneo and Duncan Idaho have a conversation that erupts into violence. Idaho is disgusted by the lesbian behavior among his Fish Speakers, but Moneo tolerantly points out that it is normal for adolescent females as well as males to have feelings of physical attraction toward members of their own sex. Moneo also accuses Duncan of adolescent behavior, and hints that this behavior is the reason he has been brought back so many times—as a test of maturity. Provoked beyond his capacity to resist, Idaho lunges at Moneo with his knife, but Moneo is so fast that he easily moves out of the way. Moneo tells a shocked Duncan that Leto has been breeding the Atreides for a long time, strengthening them in many things. Duncan is just "an older model" (318/323).

In the desert the dialogue between Leto and Siona continues. Leto tells stories and recites a poem, all in the original voices, for Siona to interpret. This she takes as another test and refuses. Leto interprets the poem for her, making it into an allegory of freedom from the past. As she tires and gets cold, Leto pulls his face partly into its cowl, creating a depression at the bottom arc of his first segment, almost like a hammock. At his suggestion, Siona curls up there and is warmed. She is constantly probing for secret knowledge of Leto. Meanwhile, back at the Citadel Moneo apologizes to Duncan for making him feel inadequate, but he also makes Hwi Noree promise not to see Duncan again.

For two full days and nights Siona has failed to seal her face mask, losing precious water with every breath. Siona is beginning to wonder if Leto can be fitted into her image of the Ultimate Tyrant because this test—learning to live with the Worm—derives from their common Fremen ancestors. Leto finally tells her about the face mask, but also asks her to command his Fish Speakers if she survives. He then offers her melange-saturated water to drink from his own body, both of them knowing full well the special susceptibility of Atreides genes. This is her choice: to die or take melange and become sensitized to the Golden Path. Siona drinks the pale blue drops that form at the edge of the curled flaps of Leto's cowl when it is rubbed. She then has a hideous apocalyptic vision of mankind's extinction at the hands of seeking machines. No ancestral presences remain in her consciousness, however. She cannot be tracked by any predator, whether human or machine. Indeed, she is not present in any of Leto's journals, though he, with the predator's necessary cruelty, has created her. Siona creates only herself, and although she still despises Leto for what he has done, Leto urges her to breed and preserve this trait for the survival of mankind. In a brief foreshadowing of what is to come, Leto suffers pain and agony as a brief rainstorm saturates the desert. He feels that he is being ripped apart. Sandtrout want to rush to the water and encapsulate it while the sandworm part of him feels the drenching wash of death, curls of blue smoke spurting from every place the rain touches him.

Siona and Leto return to the Citadel. With some bitterness, Siona accepts the command of Leto's Fish Speakers. To keep them out of danger during the wedding festivities, Siona and Duncan are to be sent to a small village of Museum Fremen at the edge of the Sareer known as Tuono, accompanied by Nayla. Unexpectedly, however, the God Emperor changes his mind about the location of his wedding from Sietch Tabr to Tuono, and this act proves to be the denouement of the novel, for Duncan and Siona are then able to plot his assassination. With the help of Nayla, who has a lasgun and who thinks it is another test of her faith to obey Siona in all things—even the murder of her God—the rebels climb a barrier wall and wait for Leto's entourage to cross a river gorge on a bridge that is part of the Royal Roadway. Before leaving his Citadel, Leto has Moneo murder Malky for his role in the attack on the Ixian Embassy. Malky has been hiding from Leto's prescient vision in an Ixian device like the no-room in which Leto's journals are recorded. Before he dies, Malky mocks the God Emperor with the fact that the secret of the Ixian device is now spread far and wide.

When Leto's procession is on the bridge, Nayla blasts the suspension cables with her lasgun, thinking that her Lord Leto will perform a miracle any moment. Instead, first Moneo, then Hwi Noree, and finally Leto all fall into the maelstrom of boiling rapids that is the Idaho River. Only Leto survives the fall, though the sandtrout have left him. Exuding blue fumes, his agonized body writhes its way along a shingle of beach and into a shallow cave. Here Nayla finds him, asking if he still lives. Duncan enters the cave in fury over Hwi Noree's death (Nayla was not instructed to kill her). Snatching the lasgun from her holster, Idaho burns her to the ground. Then he and Siona hear the God Emperor's last words as his body slowly dissolves into a bloody pulp. Leto says that nobody will find the descendants of Siona because the Oracle cannot see her. Furthermore, Leto has given them the Golden Path—a new kind of time without parallels that will always diverge. He also tells Duncan the location of his spice hoard, at Sietch Tabr. Lastly, in an enigmatic statement that is characteristic of him, he tells them both not to fear the Ixians. They can make machines, but they no longer can make *arafel*. Siona affirms to Duncan that she is the new Atreides, like Leto, but also different: "The multitude is there but I walk silently among them and no one sees me. The old images are gone and only the essence remains to light his Golden Path (409/420). Siona tells Duncan that *arafel* means the cloud darkness of holy judgment and that it's from an old story: "You'll find it all in my journals" (409/421).[3]

God Emperor closes as it had opened, with an excerpt from the writings of Hadi Benotto, this time a secret summation on the discoveries at Dar-es-Balat, made nearly two millennia after Leto's death. Ironically, she is writing the minority report to protest the editing and censorship of the journals. Apparently, too much in them threatens the status quo of the religion, called the Church of the Divided God, that has solidified around the God Emperor in the centuries since his death (we see a lot more of this religion in *Heretics of Dune*). Benotto reminds the political censors that the "poor sandworms in their Rakian Reservation" (the planet's name has gone from Dune to Arrakis to Dune, thence to Rakis) cannot yet provide an alternative to Ixian navigation machines, and that every historical reference from the Scattering and Famine Times must be taken out and reexamined. Leto has succeeded—no death can find all of humankind which has populated countless worlds. Nonetheless, there is clearly the implied threat that Benotto, and others of her persuasion, will have to be driven out from the original core of humankind because of their desire to discover new and perhaps surprising things about the universe Leto has created.

It was Herbert's desire that the reader of the Dune series would augment the story development through selected quotations from an imaginary library of the future. These selections, which precede every section and which also are sometimes sections themselves or appendices, were intended to suggest a wealth of literature pointing unmistakably to a rich culture of tradition and myth surrounding the planet Dune. The trilogy alone contains more than seventy-five such books. *Dune* is dominated by the writings of Princess Irulan, thus emphasizing her unique role in the Imperium as an official biographer and historian of Paul Atreides (*The Dune Encyclopedia* has a complete list of her writings). A similar role, that of royal scribe, is reserved for Harq-al-Ada (Farad'n) in *Children of Dune*. *Dune Messiah* is dominated by quotations from the writings of Paul Muad'Dib.

God Emperor of Dune is unique in the series, however, because almost all of the quotations are from *The Stolen Journals* (and not from the complete journals found at Dar-es-Balat). They were written by Leto to personalize himself to distant readers in the future, to make him seem less of a despot. Indeed, they show an acute awareness of the audience they are being shaped for, and for that very reason are more dialogical than some of Leto's tirades and lectures to Moneo and others in the novel. Written in the first person (the early drafts of *God Emperor* show that Herbert wrote most of the novel in the first person and left notes for himself to transcribe into the third person; material that he did not transcribe resulted in the journal quotations), they range informally and thought-provokingly over a broad range of subjects from government to prophecy to the nature of language.[4] In short, these selections are substantial enough on their own to serve as a counterpoint with which to decenter Leto's absolute authority in the novel. I believe that this is their primary function, for Leto so dominates the book that the other characters seem to exist at times only to bring out differences in him. Even in their most private thoughts they are all obsessed with the God Emperor.

This decentering, which prevents the novel from becoming absolutely monological, can be seen most clearly in Leto's remarks about language, although in another selection he remarks that he creates "a field without self or center" (304/308). Toward the end of the novel, as Leto is sensitizing Siona to the demands of the Golden Path, this selection occurs:

> The Duncans sometimes ask if I understand the exotic ideas of our past? And if I understand them, why can't I explain them? Knowledge, the Duncans believe, resides only in particulars. I try to tell them that all words are plastic. Word images begin to distort in the instant of utterance. Ideas embedded in a language require that particular language for expression. This is the very essence of the meaning within the word *exotic*. See how it begins to

distort? Translation squirms in the presence of the exotic. The Galach which I speak here imposes itself. It is an outside frame of reference, a particular system. Dangers lurk in all systems. Systems incorporate the unexamined beliefs of their creators. Adopt a system, accept its beliefs, and you help strengthen the resistance to change. Does it serve any purpose for me to tell the Duncans that there are no languages for some things? Ahhh! but the Duncans believe that all languages are mine. (336/342)

Although this passage is composed in the informal style of journal writing, it presents a number of Herbert's ideas about language. First of all, the passage opposes the linguistic system in all its abstraction, timelessness, and impersonal rules, to the individual utterance that is free to distort or blur meanings (just *how* free is another matter; there may be rules of utterance as well as lexical, syntactic, and phonetic rules). The science of linguistics has privileged the abstract study of language as a system since its inception with de Saussure, and clearly Leto is aware of how Galach—a kind of lingua franca used throughout the Imperium, similar to the role of Latin in the Middle Ages—imposes itself. But Leto does not merely repeat that opposition and its hierarchy. In fact, he clearly states the dangers of believing in systems: they strengthen the resistance to change. What is more, he seems to want to subvert that hierarchy with the notion of utterance.

An utterance is not just the opposite of language as a system, it is Leto's overall term for the duality of roles—speaking and listening—that are involved in any communicative act. Leto's Ixian machine, the dictatel, which supposedly received and encoded this passage, had to record it sequentially without the possibility of response. But when human beings (here Duncan and Leto) use language, they do so not as machines sending and receiving messages according to a code, but as two communicators engaged in active understanding: the speaker listens and the listener speaks. Any utterance, such as Duncan's question about the God Emperor's understanding of exotic ideas, and his ability to translate them, is a link in a very complexly organized chain of communication. This is so even though Leto is aware of the irony and futility of trying overtly to tell the Duncans this fact.

Secondly, Leto's utterances themselves enact an awareness of the otherness of language in general–its relationship to something outside the system which we might believe is absolute—and the otherness of given dialogic partners in particular. Leto is speaking to us of his Duncans' inability to understand that all languages are not his. On the contrary, it would seem from his remarks about the word *exotic* that the system of language imposes itself and possesses him. Galach imposes itself in the word *exotic* which in its root meaning, its "inside," means outside. But see how the word begins to blur in Leto's utterance of it, changing into its opposite. Although Leto is performing, playing with the idea of inside and outside and where we are to locate him as a speaker, this is not just a game. Leto lays bare the social means by which we appropriate words from others and make them mean what we want. He has taken the word *exotic* from Duncan and by translating it made it mean something other than what Duncan intended.

Lastly, by performing thus, he signals his own position as a speaking subject that is clearly not that of a sovereign, godlike consciousness surveying its power over language, but rather that of someone who shapes and is shaped by it in a dialogical process. Leto is decentered by his own use of language, but Leto's *Stolen Journals* (with all the ironies intended in that title) are nonetheless part of an act of authorship which created the Golden Path by appropriating the dreams and schemes of others. We might also reflect on what was said earlier about the nature of texts such as *The Stolen Journals* in the context of remarks Leto makes here about translation which "squirms" in the face of the exotic. The differences between language as a system and utterance (or discourse) determines very exactly the paradox of translation. Every system of signs (that is, every "language") can in principle be deciphered—that has been the dream of machine translation and Herbert's Ixians have certainly carried it out to the fullest extent with their dictatel machine—because there is a general logic of sign systems. Yet a text (as distinct from a system of signs) can never be fully translated because there is no text of texts, potential and unified. The nonreiterative and unique textual aspects of Leto's *Journals,* their intensely personal style, can never be fully translated. What is more unique than a fingerprint, or indeed, a voiceprint, by which the findings at Dar-es-Balat are recognized as authentic? Leto here again shows himself to be aware of the nature of textuality and authorship, as he showed himself to be with Sister Chenoeh. Consequently the belief held by the Duncans that all languages are his is true in the mechanical, and even in the semiotic (the science of signs) sense, yet it is used here by Leto to point up another one of his paradoxes.

While I am acutely aware of the fallacy of equating what a character says with what an author intends, I think that many of Herbert's ideas are incarnated in his creation, Leto II, the God Emperor of Dune, who is one of the most "exotic" science-fiction characters ever created. And insofar as we, the readers of *God Emperor of Dune,* wrest particular meanings for ourselves out of the general systems of discourse Leto deploys—whether it be politics, religion, or "metalinguistic" statements such as the passage we have just examined—we are all creators, writing the text that is our self in the language of others. I examine further the implications of this view of language, and how it helps us to situate Herbert in the history of science fiction, below in chapter seven.

Chapter Six
Heretics of Dune and *Chapterhouse: Dune*

It has been fifteen hundred years since Leto's death. Due to the Scattering and Famine Times the universe has changed profoundly. Humankind has achieved infinite diversity, inhabiting, Herbert makes clear, other universes as well. All this is according to Leto's design. However, at the core of the old Atreides Empire we find some of the same power groups vying with each other. *Heretics of Dune* focuses on the Bene Gesserit as one of the most powerful forces in this new universe, equal at least to the Spacing Guild, superior to the Fish Speaker Council (the Fish Speakers themselves are now protégés of Ix), superior by far to CHOAM, and balanced somehow with the Fabricators of Ix who have invented invisible no-ships and navigation machines, and with Bene Tleilax, which has created Face Dancers that are nearly impossible to detect (Face Dancers now sit in the highest councils of Ix and Fish Speakers, the exchange undetected) as well as techniques to capture a person's entire personality intact on the moment of death. Tleilax has been waiting in the wings for millennia to emerge as the greatest power in the universe. Now, with the return of the Lost Ones from the Scattering, and their own Face Dancers sent out among them, the time seems ripe. No legal system could bind such a complexity into a whole and this fact has brought up a constant need for arbiters with clout. The Reverend Mothers have naturally fallen into this role within the economic web. They hold authority in this area despite Tleilax-grown melange that has broken the Rakian monopoly on spice, just as Ixian navigation machines have broken the Guild monopoly on space travel, because they have a formidable knowledge of the myths and customs of other cultures, an outgrowth of their Missionaria Protectiva.

However, although the Bene Gesserit remains the most powerful and enduring missionary force known, the Tyrant's achievement in religious management has bested them. Leto is worshipped in various ways throughout the universe, even, we discover, by the Tleilaxu, who hold him to be a prophet of God. His many Dreaming Minds in the sandworms of Rakis are still an oracular force holding the Bene Gesserit in bondage. Many in the Sisterhood fear his return, but nonetheless a plot is being set in motion, known as the ghola project, to destroy the Tyrant's control forever. Of course, the complete design, which involves the destruction of Rakis and the capturing of one of the giant sandworms to start a new desert on the Bene Gesserit home world of Chapterhouse, is not fully revealed until the very end. Because of so many secrets in the narrative, including the real nature of the Duncan Idaho ghola and the Tleilaxu axolotl tanks (which turn out to be not tanks at all but gross mounds of female flesh), the reader feels caught up in a swirl of events, sensing a wholeness from clues provided, but unable to discern a complete pattern, like many of the characters who reflect on their roles within the Bene Gesserit plan.

Heretics opens on the planet Gammu, formerly the Harkonnen planet of Giedi Prime, where the ghola project is headquartered. Reverend Mother Lucilla is visiting the commander of Gammu Keep, Reverend Mother Schwangyu. Lucilla is a sexual Imprinter, a brown-haired charmer with full breasts and a motherly disposition, who is to bind the adolescent ghola to the Sisterhood at the appropriate time, if he lives. The previous eleven gholas have been killed by unknown assassins. We learn later that the Tleilaxu have themselves been killing them to control the timing of the ghola project. Reverend Mother Schwangyu makes no secret about her disagreement with Mother Superior Taraza, the architect of the plan. The ghola project touches an old nerve among many Sisters. The possibility, even remote, that they might arouse another Kwisatz Haderach sends shudders of angry fear throughout the ranks. And to meddle with the wormbound remnants of the Tyrant seems dangerous in the extreme to her. Lucilla does not know the entire design of the project, just her role as Imprinter, but Schwangyu tells her of a female child named Sheeana (a modern form of Siona) Brugh on Rakis who can control the giant worms.

When the time is right, presumably when Sheeana has passed through puberty under Bene Gesserit tutelage, the ghola is to be sent to Rakis. In the meantime, however, he is being trained by Miles Teg, an Atreides who resembles the first Leto, grandfather of the Tyrant. This resemblance is to help him trigger the Duncan's memories at the appropriate moment. Teg is a fascinating character, a legendary

Mentat-Warrior over three hundred years old who is bound in loyalty to serve the Bene Gesserit. In fact, he was once the Supreme Bashar of all their forces, and he has now been called out of retirement to be the Duncan's weaponsmaster. In the agony of torture later in the novel he is thrust over the threshold of mentat-consciousness into something like a kwisatz haderach. The ghola is a replica of the original Duncan Idaho, except that his reflexes have been speeded up to match those born in these times. Once again, Herbert brings back a favorite character and we witness the drama of his recovery of the original Duncan's memories. He is deeply and hatefully suspicious of the Bene Gesserit designs on him, however, and the Tleilaxu have made some changes in his cellular inheritance not requested by the Sisterhood. It turns out that the Tleilaxu have been using the gholas as testing models. All of their leaders are gholas. They have had axolotl tank immortality since the days of the first Duncan and now they possess memories of serial lives too. This Duncan is a cellular mix, and indeed he does later recall *all* of the memories of his previous selves.

The early chapters also introduce another Atreides, Darwi Odrade, who is Senior Security Mother on the ghola project. Odrade has born nineteen children for the Bene Gesserit, each child by a different father, yet this essential service to the Sisterhood has not grossened her flesh. Her features still convey the natural hauteur of the Atreides genes. Although she possesses a prescient instinct for detecting threats to the Sisterhood, and was a younger classmate of Taraza (they are still known as "Dar and Tar"), the Sisterhood has never trusted the wild influence of her genetic line that produced the Kwisatz Haderach and the Tyrant. (Odrade's Other Memories, though, are no longer selectively filtered to keep the breeding records secret; it is an easy matter for her to find out that Miles Teg is her father.) Consequently, she also is not privy to the whole design of the ghola project. It remains a puzzle to her until she receives Taraza's memories when she dies at the end of the novel, when Odrade becomes the Mother Superior and later the main character of *Chapterhouse: Dune.* Nonetheless, Odrade recognizes the necessity for assigned roles conducted within separate cells, for the Bene Gesserit have always seen themselves as permanent revolutionaries: "It [their political organization] was an ancient design copied from secret revolutionary societies."[1] So despite the seeming closeness of Dar and Tar at times, the survival of the Bene Gesserit is the most important thing. Taraza would not hesitate to eliminate Odrade if the situation warranted such action. And only Taraza knows the entire design.

A major threat to the ghola project are forces from out of the Scattering, the Lost Ones, particularly descendants of the Tleilaxu deployed by wildly brutal women calling themselves Honored Matres. Orange-eyed huntresses, the Matres use a more virulent form of Bene Gesserit sexual bonding techniques to extend the power of females over males. The Matres can deploy the entire arsenal of the Tantric *ars erotica,* and in addition are Herbert's means to introduce the science of sexuality, and sexual discourse in general, into the Dune series.[2] Terms such as "orgasmic platform" and "vaginal pulsing," which occur in the conversations with and about them, seem right out of a college textbook on sexology. Above all, the Matres demonstrate how the techniques of power have operated on sexuality in our age. Indeed, in ideological terms the battles that are fought in the book center around "the great problem of the human universe" (455/446), sexual energy, and how to manage procreation. The Bene Gesserit feel compelled to call the Honored Matres "whores" (while they themselves have long been called "witches" due to their use of the Voice by everyone from Duncan Idaho to the Baron Harkonnen to the Tleilaxu—all males, of course) because they ape Bene Gesserit ways, putting themselves and their sexuality at the center of worship. To the Sisterhood they seem crude and naive, hardly understanding the forces that they ride upon and that they could unleash destructively. The Tleilaxu, under the leadership of their Mahai, Tylwyth Waff, have already encountered the Honored Matres and have managed to replace one of them with a Face Dancer, learning in the process something of this sexual knowledge which the Tleilaxu have incorporated into the latest ghola. So the Duncan, programmed as he is to kill his Imprinter, whether "witch" or "whore," is a sexually loaded weapon. Knowing the past history and the attractiveness of the Duncan to women, the Tleilaxu probably hope also that he will use this knowledge of their sexuality to dominate them in turn.

Because so many diverse forces from the Scattering have assembled on Gammu, Taraza tells Miles Teg that the ghola must be awakened at the first opportunity, despite his objections and a report from Lucilla that he is still too young (he is sixteen). In the meantime, Odrade is dispatched to Rakis where she will oversee the induction of Sheeana, whom the priests of Church of Shai-Hulud consider to be a Holy Child. A great deal of satire is focused on these credulous—and murderous—priests, who are concerned only with their own authority and institutional survival. Herbert gets the euphemistic language of this priestly caste down perfectly, as when they refer to the practice of sacrificing human beings to the sandworms as "translation." Because she can control the worms, the priests are terrified of Sheeana, but also troubled because she refers to their god, Shai-Hulud, as Shaitan. The sly priests and their intrigues are kept at bay by Hedley Tuek, the High Priest, who seems genuinely concerned about her welfare. Sheeana herself is a very clever orphan of the desert who senses the powers of her position early on. By the time Odrade arrives, she has spontaneously developed control of the Voice, but is bored with chastising dim-witted priests who keep trying to trap her into committing heresy. She is delighted with Odrade, who she thinks will be an interesting opponent. An affection between the two develops quickly.

It is not long before the Tleilaxu and their Face Dancers mount attacks on both the Rakian temple complex where Sheeana is housed and the Gammu Keep. Both gambits fail, at least initially, but the Tleilaxu have managed to subvert Schwangyu into a pact with them. In order to make the "dirty Tleilaxu" pay for these attacks, Taraza meets with Master Waff, forcing him to strike a deal: in exchange for the secrets they have learned about the Honored Matres, the Bene Gesserit agree to offer the Tleilaxu some of their prize human bloodlines, on condition that the Bene Gesserit breeding mothers have unfettered access to the Tleilaxu genetic laboratories or a fully operational axolotl tank. They agree to complete the bargain on Rakis, Taraza having convinced Waff that the Bene Gesserit share some of their religious beliefs (the Tleilaxu are both Zensunni and Sufi). In effect, Taraza is creating an alliance between the Sisterhood and the Tleilaxu, but on her terms. Waff does not suspect that he is bait in a larger trap about to be sprung on Rakis.

Waff arrives on Rakis and has an interview with Hedley Tuek (a descendant, apparently, of Esmar Tuek in *Dune*) and Odrade. Waff tries to kill them both, but only succeeds in killing the High Priest, who is later replaced by a Face Dancer with Odrade's approval. In forming an alliance with the Bene Gesserit, the Tleilaxu secretly hope to control Rakis. The Shariat, their religious government, would then be ascendant at last with the Bene Gesserit as missionaries converting the many peoples of the Scattering to the Great Belief. In the Bene Gesserit design, on the other hand, the game has become very delicate. For generations now they have held out to the Rakian priesthood the bait of a Bene Gesserit alliance. But now the Tleilaxu must consider that *they* have been chosen instead of the priests because the Sisterhood shares the Tleilaxu Great Belief. Odrade's on-scene decision to allow a Face Dancer to impersonate the High Priest, however, really puts the Tleilaxu into an untenable position. The impersonator could be exposed, and the Bene Tleilax plunged into a sink of hatred. Odrade thus has composed a three-cornered alliance, allowing the priests to think every Reverend Mother will take the Oath of Subservience to the Divided God. Of course, the Tleilaxu see the chance to monopolize melange, controlling at last the one source independent of them.

For her part, Taraza is pleased with the outcome of Odrade's decision. She has never considered the priesthood to be a central problem. Already caught up in religion, the priests can be manipulated by religion. They see the Bene Gesserit chiefly as a power that could enforce their dogma. It is a bait that blinds them. Taraza is much more worried about the fate of the ghola project on Gammu for she has not had any report from there in three months. Taraza has dispatched Burzmali, the Bashar's favorite student, to find out what has happened to Miles Teg and the ghola, but he sends no favorable report either.

On Gammu, Teg, Lucilla, and the ghola have found sanctuary in an old Harkonnen no-globe. There they wait for an opportunity to escape while Schwangyu searches feverishly for them. Teg, however, has very cleverly hidden their tracks by simulating the marks of a no-ship's takeoff burn. Should Schwangyu dare bring in a prescient searcher to follow Duncan's tracks (because Duncan alone among them has no Siona blood in his ancestry to shield him), all of the marks would agree that they had fled off-planet.[3] During the three months Teg decides on his own to block Lucilla's seductive efforts and to awaken the ghola. Every Mentat projection Teg can make about Duncan's safety and sanity requires the awakening of his pre-ghola memories ahead of any Imprint by Lucilla. Lucilla is furious at the outcome, for the fully restored Duncan now is very much her equal in the amorous battle, playing a delaying game with his seductress. This Duncan is immune to the powers of the Voice, and has been instructed by Teg, whose mother was a Bene Gesserit who taught him many things about the Sisterhood forbidden for males to know.

On Rakis Odrade is attempting to find out more about the hidden language used between Sheeana and the worms, which is encoded in the dance she performs. To that end she takes Sheeana and Waff on an expedition into the desert. Sheeana quickly calls up a worm and they ride off on it. Eventually the worm takes them to Sietch Tabr buried in the sand. Using her prescient sense, Odrade discovers a long-hidden spice hoard of Leto's together with a message he has left for them. Emblazoned on the stone walls of the hidden entrance to the hoard is the word *arafel* (variously translated as "the cloud darkness at the end of the universe," and "the cloud darkness of holy judgement"; as previously explained, *arafel* is the biblical Hebrew word for "cloud" and is used in the book of Exodus to describe the cloud from which God speaks when he delivers the ten commandments to Moses on Mount Sinai), which leads Odrade to several other messages on the walls of the sietch cave, including one that says that a Reverend Mother will read his words. Odrade realizes that the Tyrant is part of the design, having sent a message down the eons to the Bene Gesserit of today. The messages are mainly probing questions: "Why did the Sisterhood not build the Golden Path?" "What if you no longer hear the music of life?" "With whom do you ally?" "How will you meet your end? As no more than a secret society?" (310–11/301–2). Because Leto uses the phrase "noble purpose" in one of these questions, Odrade now feels that she understands all of Taraza's design. The Bene Gesserit, just as Taraza had predicted, need not fear to reawaken the Tyrant. In fact, Odrade interprets these writings as inviting them to join Leto—the noble design involving the survival of mankind has been started and must be completed even if it means the death of the Sisterhood.

On Gammu, Burzmali finally locates Teg. Unfortunately, in a skirmish that begins almost immediately after the group emerges from the no-globe, Teg is taken prisoner by the Honored Matres, though Duncan and Lucilla escape while he fights a diverting action with an old Harkonnen lasgun. Many Face Dancers die in the attack, and some Masters as well, because they want to take him alive. With the help of an underground movement on Gammu made up of people of the Scattering opposed to the Honored Matres, Burzmali and Lucilla enter the capital city of Ysai disguised as an Honored Matre prostitute and her customer. Duncan is disguised as a Tleilaxu Master and is conveyed separately. People working for the Matres torture Teg with a device called a T-probe that can "read" everything about a person, even unconscious memories. Gradually, however, Teg's Mentat awareness matches that of the machine (it learns him but he learns it as well) until at last he becomes aware of the fact that he can move with tremendous speed. He easily breaks the straps tying him to the T-probe and kills his torturers before they even begin to register surprise. Later, Teg discovers that the crisis he passed through under torture has thrust him over the threshold into a new reality and into another dimension of human possibility.[4] Driven by necessity and the wild genes in his Atreides ancestry, he has developed a mildly prescient double vision that tells him what to anticipate from every moment within the range of his senses. The most extraordinary thing about Teg's new awareness, however, is that the no-ships ringing Gammu are now visible to him. Many have sought a way to nullify the Ixian no-ship's invisibility, and Teg has found it. After another encounter with the Honored Matres, in which he moves like a blur slaughtering scores of them and their minions, Teg links up with some old veterans who had fought with him once. They capture a no-ship and head for Rakis where Taraza has recently arrived for the final battle.

In a related subplot Burzmali and Lucilla meet up with Duncan, who has been captured by an Honored Matre postulant named Murbella. Lucilla convinces Murbella that she outranks her, and Murbella reluctantly turns the ghola over to her authority. The sexual jousting continues, though, Duncan using his sexual techniques on Murbella until he overcomes the response pattern planted in him to kill his Imprinter, recovering his serial memories and becoming the male equivalent of an Honored Matre in the process. Not only Murbella but all the Honored Matres have been warned that there is a ghola armed with forbidden knowledge by the Tleilaxu. That ghola must be killed at all costs, but Murbella is now so sexually bonded to Duncan that she cannot accomplish his murder, although she tries. The last thing she hears before Lucilla knocks her unconscious is that this ghola is going to Rakis. Later we find out that she is pregnant and that naturally the Bene Gesserit will want the child for their own breeding program.

Although the Honored Matres greatly outnumber the Bene Gesserit forces, the resistance Teg has planned for the battle creates hysteria among them, especially when they are made to believe that the ghola is there. Not only do they counterattack, they eventually resort to sterilization procedures. Most of Rakis becomes a charred ruin. There is little likelihood that any humans, sandworms, or sandtrout have survived. Teg himself dies in the battle, as does Taraza, but not before she gives her memories to Darwi Odrade in a Bene Gesserit ritual, in effect making her the next Mother Superior. With Taraza's memories Odrade is able to review the entire course of the ghola project and to assess how well the Sisterhood has survived. Taraza had indeed played a dangerous game, with the future of the entire Sisterhood hanging in the balance. She had carefully timed the leaking of the word to the

Honored Matres that the Tleilaxu had built dangerous abilities into the ghola. And the attack on Gammu Keep confirmed that the information had reached its source. The brutal nature of that attack, though, had warned Taraza that she had little time. The Honored Matres would be sure to assemble forces for the total destruction of Gammu—just to kill that one ghola. So much depended on Teg, who changed Taraza's design by allowing the ghola to escape from Rakis with Odrade. Teg knew that the Sisterhood would need Duncan Idaho's new talents to counter the Honored Matres. He was no longer merely bait for the destruction of Rakis.

Although many in the Sisterhood have dissented from Taraza's plan (notably Bellonda, a sister who has a larger role in *Chapterhouse*), arguing that Leto was laying another trap for the Bene Gesserit on Rakis, events seem to bear out Taraza's view of things. The Honored Matres are bound by no noble purpose in preserving the species. In fact, they trade in forgetfulness, having not the least awareness of the Tyrant's continuing viselike hold on human destiny nor of the need to break that hold. As Odrade tells Sheeana, "They ignore the species at its work . . . The Tyrant certainly knew about it. What was his Golden Path but a vision of sexual forces at work recreating humankind endlessly" (451–52 /442)? The Bene Gesserit have made a prime acquisition in Sheeana, for she understands, albeit unconsciously in the ritual of her dances, the language of the sandworms, one of which Odrade has gotten aboard the no-ship on which she escapes the destruction of Rakis. The worm will be taken to Chapterhouse where it will help create a new desert ecology and evolve under the watchful eyes of the Sisterhood, there being then no need to find a desert planet for it. By the time the worms reach sufficient numbers to be an influence once more, humankind will have gone its own way beyond Leto: "We'll be too numerous by then, doing too many different things on our own. No single force will rule all of our futures completely, never again" (279/270). Looking down at the cargo bay of the no-ship where the worm lies, Odrade muses that Leto must have wanted this to happen, must have wanted out, after what he did. There is no answer from the worm, but we are fairly sure that Odrade has recovered more of the Tyrant's design than anyone else in this book.

At any rate *Heretics* closes on Chapterhouse, the Bene Gesserit home planet where the Sisterhood, through archival analysis of historical precedents, makes the following predictions of "the punishments" the various power groups will endure: those assemblages of humans who allied themselves with the Honored Matres are in for some shocks. Ix will certainly overextend itself because they have not the slightest appreciation of how competition from the Scattering will crush them (the Lost Ones have developed their own varieties of no-ships).[5] The Guild will be shunted aside and made to pay dearly for its melange and its machinery now that Rakis, its only source, has been destroyed. Guild and Ix, thrown together, will fall together. The Fish Speakers can be mostly ignored. Satellites of Ix, they are already fading into a past that humans will abandon. And the Tleilaxu in the Bene Gesserit analysis have succumbed to the wiles of the Honored Matres in trying to learn their secrets. Besides, the Sisterhood already has the key to the axolotl tanks, and it is only a matter of time before they use this technology to produce melange from the human body. Further analysis of the cell samples taken from Sheeana reveal that the "proof of Siona" is there. She has the ancestry that shields her from prescience and can leave the no-ship. The cell studies of the ghola, on the other hand, say that he is a mixture of many Idaho gholas—some descendants of Siona. Odrade decides that Duncan must remain confined while the Sisters prepare for "the long night of the whores" (476/466).

Much of the narrative counterpoint in this, the fifth installment of Herbert's ecological fugue, comes from heretical discourse. Every major character in the book gives voice to it, lending the word a very fluid, "polyphonic" quality. *Heretics* opens with Schwangyu's open revolt against a Reverend Mother Superior, which is reflected or "voiced" through Lucilla's consciousness. It is she who calls Schwangyu a heretic, though she wonders how there could be heretical movements among people such as the Bene Gesserit who hold a profoundly manipulative attitude toward all things religious (11/3). By contrast the Rakian priests are quick to attack any group that denies the centrality of their religion, but they are also internally divided into factions each accusing the other of heresy with regard to the meaning and significance of Sheeana's, the Holy Child's, pronouncements about their Divided God. Heresies, it seems, are named after the hapless priest who first utters them. The "Dromind heresy," for example, suggested that Sheeana be studied scientifically (110/103). It is not long before Dromind is "translated to the Mouth of God" for speaking such a heresy (Herbert's verbal irony is never more in evidence than when he is dealing with professional or bureaucratic jargons). The Tleilaxu also take the purity of their religion very seriously, and can hardly bear the pollution that contact with outsiders, or "powindahs," brings to them. (A visit to the Tleilaxu core planet of Bandalong, voiced through the mind of Tylwyth Waff, provides Herbert with an occasion to introduce some twenty new words describing the religious world of the Tleilaxu.) Both groups are necessarily upset by the spread of a heretical religious document known as *The Atreides Manifesto* which argues that the Rakian religion is only one among many other viable ones, that God and all His works are no more than human creations, that prescience is a belief that stagnates the mind of the believer, and argues generally against the idea of a True Religion—all of this, undeniably authentic, from the family that produced the God Emperor.

The author of *The Atreides Manifesto* (some selections from which appear at the head of sections of the novel), and the source of the mischief, is none other than Darwi Odrade, who is something of a heretic herself because she secretly believes in, and longs for, love. Love is probably the ultimate Bene Gesserit heresy. Jessica, the reader may remember, betrayed the Sisterhood by giving her Duke a son because she loved him. That son was Paul Atreides, the Kwisatz Haderach, who brought much pain to the Sisterhood through his son Leto II. Odrade is given to daydreaming about the mother figure she lost as a young child. Sibia, so the woman was named, committed the heresy of loving the child as her own and thus had to be removed. Odrade wants to be loved by her father Teg also, and thereby somehow to create a nuclear family. Years of Bene Gesserit psychoanalysis have not removed these desires either. Teg's mother, a Bene Gesserit herself, had been in Taraza's words "a wise woman but another heretic," in teaching him more than she was told to teach him about the Sisterhood (153/145). After Teg's death, Odrade is very proud of him, calling him "The Great Heretic" (476/466) because this Mentat philosopher has chewed deep into everything the Sisterhood had accepted about itself, leaving data about the Honored Matres in his "Last Will and Testament" aboard the no-ship. Chapterhouse requires nothing less than a complete revision of all its historical records due to his writings.

Chapterhouse: Dune

Teg returns in *Chapterhouse* as a ghola (actually a clone) grown from the fingernail scrapings Odrade obtained from him at their farewell meeting before the destruction of Rakis. Odrade openly quips about presiding at the birth of her own father. The Bene Gesserit have lost their repugnance toward Tleilaxu axolotl tanks, and toward many other previous anathemas—even toward cyborgs, the intermingling of human and machine—in the interest of survival and in fulfilling their quest for the grail of human maturity. Odrade wants to make more changes in the Sisterhood, changes she hopes will enable them to survive in these "interesting" times. The universe is now beset by Honored Matres and other forces. It is a universe of scattered planets peopled mostly by humans who want to live out their lives in peace—accepting Bene Gesserit guidance in some places, squirming under Honored Matre suppression in many regions, mostly hoping to govern themselves as best they can, always the perennial dream of democracy. There is really no market left, no central bourse, where the Bene Gesserit might exchange their talents. CHOAM's tightly bound trading network of the Old Empire is no more. A species of subterranean webworks still exists, but it is extremely loose, based on old compromises and temporary agreements, resembling "an old garment with frayed edges and patched holes."[6] One of the surprises to come out of this webwork is an old alliance the Sisterhood had made with the Hebrew nation, gone underground centuries ago to avoid continuing pogroms, yet still carrying on their religious beliefs. In a related subplot on Gammu, involving the death of Lucilla after she flees the destruction of the planet Lampadas—the Bene Gesserit's most prized school—by the Honored Matres, Rebecca, daughter of a rabbi, in fact becomes the first wild Reverend Mother to be seen since the days of Dune when she receives Lucilla's Other Memories from that world.

There are numerous unknowns, however, among the people returning from the Scattering. We find out very little about the origins of the Honored Matres except that Leto's Fish Speakers and Reverend Mothers in extremis had formed them. But the Fish Speaker democracy under Leto has become an autocracy under the Honored Matres, who emphasize the planting of unconscious compulsions with their T-probes, cellular induction, and sexual prowess. The Matres are themselves fleeing from another mysterious power called by them the Ones With Many Faces. Herbert gives us a segment narrated from their point of view only at the very end of the novel. They are offshoots of the Tleilaxu Face Dancers sent out in the Scattering and have become almost godlike because of their capacity to assume the persona of whomever they kill—and they have been doing this for centuries, capturing Mentats and Tleilaxu Masters and whatever else they could assimilate, until now they play with whole planets and civilizations. They are weirdly benign when they first appear in the visions of Duncan Idaho as a calm elderly couple working in a flower garden, trying to capture him in their net. Futars—humans crossed with hunting animals and apparently designed to hunt and kill Honored Matres—may be one of *their* creations.

The Matres are led by Dama, "the Spider Queen," as she is called by the Sisterhood, in the center of her web on the planet Junction. With her eyes that flame orange when she is angered, the Great Honored Matre is a much more overtly sinister character—indeed right out of Flash Gordon—than are the unknown Face Dancers, especially when she gloatingly picks off, planet by planet, the Bene Gesserit strongholds with arrogant self-assurance. Dama knows that it is only a matter of time before she finds the Sisterhood's sanctuary on Chapterhouse. On that planet, Odrade knows this fact as well, which comes to her in a terrible recurring dream. But she is not without a plan. Her first priority is trying to get as many Bene Gesserit cells as possible off the planet in a second Scattering, sent to destinations no one on Chapterhouse could know. As the novel progresses, they go flying away in their no-ships, a stock of sandtrout in their holds, Bene Gesserit traditions, learning, and memories as a guide.

But Odrade also knows that the Sisterhood had done this long ago in the first Scattering and none have come back or sent a message. Only the Honored Matres have returned, and they are a terrible, blindly suicidal distortion of the Sisterhood. Therefore, Odrade has other alternative plans, revolving around the reincarnated Teg (whom she has played mother to), Duncan Idaho, Murbella, and Sheeana. There is also the last surviving Tleilaxu Master, Scytale, or rather his ghola, who is kept a virtual prisoner aboard the same no-ship as Duncan and Murbella. No Tleilaxu planet has escaped the fate of Dune, and Scytale has asked for protection from Matres who have destroyed his entire civilization. Even Duncan Idaho is willing to admire the awesome scope of the Tleilaxu actions. They investigated a cosmos no one but the Bene Gesserit had ever dared touch. That the Bene Tleilax did this for selfish reasons does not subtract from it in Duncan's eyes. The endless rebirths of the Tleilaxu Masters to him, a ghola, seem a reward worthy of daring. With their Face Dancer servants to copy any life, any mind, the Tleilaxu had hoped to conquer the universe, but now that dream seems gone forever. Scytale does not figure much in the action of *Chapterhouse.* He is mainly a source of information about the technology of the axolotl tanks. Unknown to anyone but himself, however, Scytale has implanted in his breast, as all Masters did, a surprising resource—a nullentropy capsule preserving the seeds of a multitude: fellow Masters of the central kehl, Face Dancers, technical specialists, the original Duncan Idaho, Paul Atreides and his beloved Chani, Thufir Hawat, Gurney Halleck, the Fremen Naib Stilgar . . . and enough potential servants and slaves to populate a Tleilaxu universe. Since Scytale escapes with this resource still intact and undiscovered at the end of *Chapterhouse,* we may speculate that Herbert in using this character was allowing himself the possibility of re-creating the original cast of Dune on some other world in a further volume.

At any rate, Odrade realizes that if Teg's original memories are restored, then the Sisterhood will once more have the finest Mentat Bashar to serve them, a military genius who drove the Matres to a berserk response on Dune. Teg is still a young boy when Odrade decides to revive his memories, using Duncan Idaho. But Duncan, remembering the pain Teg caused him when he restored Duncan's memories, has a better idea. He suspects that Teg's heretic mother had planted a hypno-induction in him to block any Bene Gesserit Imprinter. The sexual advances of an Imprinter might therefore be a gentler shock with which to awaken Teg. Duncan turns out to be right, and Teg is awakened to his past self as Bashar by Sheeana, who has learned Imprinting techniques from Murbella, although she is immune to them herself.

As readers of *Heretics* will remember, the original plan had been to bond Sheeana to Duncan. The Sisterhood would then control him and he could control her. Of course, this did not turn out as planned. Duncan discovered a deep mutual addiction, or "sexual collision," as he calls it, with Murbella, a woman once trained by the Honored Matres. Murbella has now produced several children for the Bene Gesserit during the years of their confinement to the no-ship. She is still on probation as a somewhat dangerous and dimly understood product of the Matres, but Odrade hopes that her incredible speed and bonding techniques can be added to the Sisterhood's repertoire. After her latest child is delivered, she is scheduled to endure the Spice Agony and become a full Reverend Mother—an experience that will make her both Matre and Mother, with the latter providing some balance for the former's violently chaotic tendencies.

For years now Duncan has been training men in sexual bonding techniques, later polished by Sheeana at the Desert Station, to be sent out to plague the Honored Matres. These men taunt the hunters. However, Duncan understands that the Sisterhood is his only protection at the moment, and that it is a shaky one at best. There are those, like

Bellonda the Archivist, herself a Mentat like him, who want the ghola destroyed because they fear he may be another Kwisatz Haderach. Odrade prefers to keep Duncan alive as a stud in the Sisterhood's breeding program and as a possible weaponsmaster in a military showdown with the Matres. He also understands that once Murbella becomes a Reverend Mother, she will no longer be bonded to him. During most of the novel he is busy exploring his strange new visions of the elderly couple behind the net, with his growing powers of mental computation, and with finding ways to steal the no-ship and to escape, with the connivance of Sheeana. Although he is under constant observation in the no-ship, he has managed to teach her a secret hand-talk.

Sheeana is not happy with what the Sisterhood has planned for her either. The cult of Sheeana has spread all over the Old Empire and beyond, carried by surviving priests from Rakis. The Bene Gesserit's Missionaria Protectiva wants to use this "myth power," once the worms have arisen in the rapidly developing desert on Chapterhouse. Once the worms arise, the Sisterhood is prepared to launch Sheeana—providing she can still control the worms—on an unsuspecting humanity prepared for religious adoration, the myth of Shai-Hulud having become real in her person. Sheeana had supposedly died in the destruction of Dune and is now a powerful spirit in the pantheon of the oppressed. Thus does the Bene Gesserit plan to use the myths of Dune as a weapon. Although Sheeana has become a Reverend Mother—the youngest ever to attain that status—and is promoted to the Council by Odrade, she has great misgivings about this plan because she senses the hubris of it. It is the very kind of religious implant Muad'Dib and his Tyrant son set loose upon an unsuspecting humankind. While she knows that her name has become a shining light in the darkness of Honored Matre oppression, she also knows how easy it is for that light to become a consuming flame. Sheeana wants no jihads undertaken in her name. The worms eventually do occur in the desert, and Sheeana can control them, but she wants only to escape from Chapterhouse because she believes it is a death trap not only for its inhabitants but also for Bene Gesserit dreams: "My migration will seek the new. But . . . I must find a planet with moons [i.e., like Dune]" (431).

This much of Odrade's plan then goes awry when Sheeana escapes at the end of the novel. Most of what Odrade plans, however, comes off brilliantly, including her surprising transformation of the Bene Gesserit itself through Murbella. When Teg is fully restored to his Bashar identity, even though physically he is just barely an adolescent, and with Duncan as weaponsmaster, Odrade daringly decides not to wait for the Matres to find her, but to attack them instead. She plans a feint at Gammu first, then, when the remaining Matre supporters have escaped to Junction, an all-out attack on that planet. She goes to Junction herself to distract the Spider Queen at the core of her web with a ruse of Bene Gesserit submission, having prepared herself to die by sharing her Other Memories with Murbella, who earlier has passed through the Spice Agony, and Sheeana. Odrade does die in the ensuing conflict, but Murbella manages to receive her last memories and thereby supplant the current Great Honored Matre, Logno (who kills Dama in a power struggle during the battle), becoming the leader of both female societies. She commands by tying a Gordian knot of discourse between them: "It was Great Honored Matre giving orders but those who leaped to obey sensed the Other in her" (439).

Perhaps, as Odrade-Within hopes, this cross-fertilization of the two female societies will create a hybrid vigor, Honored Matres slipping into Bene Gesserit ways, until, one day, there will be no Honored Matres, only Reverend Mothers with improved reflexes and augmented knowledge of sexuality. But Murbella has her work cut out for her, and some are not staying around to find out the results. Sheeana, together with a group of Reverend Mothers who think that the Sisterhood has changed too much, provide Duncan with the key to reinstate the no-ship's flight controls. The ship vanishes into space, taking with it Scytale, some Futars who have sought an alliance with the Bene Gesserit, Teg, and the rabbi and his daughter Rebecca. Duncan sees the net of Face Dancers growing stronger around him and dumps from the ship's computers navigation segments and nullfields. The ship escapes the Face Dancers, lurching into foldspace. It emerges in a place where Idaho recognizes none of the visible star patterns: "We're an unidentifiable ship in an unidentifiable universe . . Isn't that what we wanted?" (454). The Dune series has gone from Muad'Dib to Tyrant to Honored Matres to Bene Gesserit. Will the next phase be a Sheeana future, which Murbella thinks will be "a bitter medicine" to the Bene Gesserit (457)? We are not certain, but if so, then some will choke on that medicine, but the survivors may, Herbert tells us, create interesting patterns.

Chapterhouse: Dune provides us with a richly detailed look at two female societies, their discourses and social practices, and the conflicts between them. The ecology of the planet Chapterhouse is the most detailed, as is the Bene Gesserit stewardship over it. Quite early in the novel we are immersed in discussions of the misleading and dangerous notion of ownership, the nature of the "ecological circle" and symbiosis, and how best to manage the resources of this planet that the Sisterhood is trying to transform into a desert, a new Dune. The society that we find is equally based on ecological principles. Every Sister has her niche in the political ecology of the Sisterhood which, despite its secrecy and use of surveillance techniques, has some democratic features, such as the Convocation and the Council, which are depicted here for the first time. Even dead Reverend Mothers are put to use. They are buried standing up in the orchards to fertilize the fruit-bearing trees. The Honored Matres, by contrast, are a totally autocratic society that depends on fear, suspicion, and sexual dominance over others to accomplish its goals in the area of power. Looking only outward, they try to control the universe, not balance with it. Unfortunately, we are never given a glimpse of their home world, but compared to the frugal and ecologically oriented Sisterhood, they are a vision of excess and total expenditure. The luxury that the Honored Matres enjoy on Gammu is made evident late in *Heretics.* In *Chapterhouse* they are involved in conquering an entire planet because of the beautiful "soostones" that occur there. This luxury is kept from the lower classes of their society behind a barrier of what they like to call protective ignorance: "We teach that new knowledge can be dangerous . . . All new knowledge is non-survival! (*Heretics,* 444/435). What Teg discovers on Gammu, however, is that they are so cynical and depraved that nothing is expected to surprise them, nothing can be truly new for them. Still, they plot and devise, hoping that *this* extreme will produce the remembered thrill. Dama in *Chapterhouse* sleeps with her captive Futar, whom she ordinarily keeps in a cage. They know, of course, that new experiences based on this kind of degradation will not succeed in producing that thrill, and they expect to carry away from the experience only more burning rage out of which to fashion another attempt at the unreachable.

Of course, there are similarities between the two societies as well. Both societies, for example, depend on addiction for their survival. In the case of the Bene Gesserit it is melange addiction, and for the Matres it is sexual bondage (though apparently they do not bond one another in this manner). But what is a master without a slave to recognize her? The flaw of dependency in their sexual economy is quite obvious to the Sisterhood, who aim at removing dependencies. True, the Bene Gesserit do not rule themselves by crude sexual power and "orgasmic amplification" either, but rather by the authority of their Mother Superior who is elected—they preserve key elements of a "jury-monitored democracy in original form" (*Chapterhouse,* 367)—and by rites of sharing Other Memories that bind them into a kind of family and to a larger awareness of their place in human history and evolution. They do not trade in forgetfulness. Nonetheless, both groups do use sexual bonding techniques to insinuate themselves into power situations, although the Bene Gesserit prefer to remain operative behind the scenes of power (this may indeed be a traditional role for women in relation to power, but that is another matter). Perhaps the most striking similarity lies in the fact that both societies produce rage in their members. The rage of Dama was previously mentioned. Odrade in *Heretics* becomes aware of this rage in herself and is able to detect it in Taraza even before she shares Other Memories with her. At the core of Taraza is "a giant howl of rage against the uses others had made of her life. The power of that suppressed rage was daunting even though it could never be expressed in a way that vented it" (*Heretics,* 354/345). The Sisterhood, by never allowing this rage to heal, feeds on its power, although the institution itself, primarily through the mechanism of the Spice Agony, is able to direct such rage along constructive lines. Love, and intimately personal relations, are never allowed to develop in either female society.

On a simple level, the level of our immediate and probably mostly unconscious response, Herbert is deploying two male archetypes of the feminine—the witch and the whore (apparently virginity has no interest at all for him). But considered as one long dialogical novel, *Heretics* and *Chapterhouse* together raise these archetypes to the conscious level of rational analysis in the conversations that occur between representatives of the two societies. Both societies seem perfectly aware of what psychological mechanisms are involved in the projection of unconscious images and try to use this knowledge as a blind to the other. The Great Honored Matre, for example, is delighted that Odrade thinks of her as "the Spider Queen" (*Chapterhouse,* 17), and the Bene Gesserit have fostered an image of themselves as witches for millenia. What Herbert's ultimate intention was in playing with such powerful archetypes of the male psyche I can only guess at here. But any novel based on dialogical principles of relationship to an Other would sooner or later have to confront the nature and social position of women, whose voices have long been excluded from male-dominated discourses. This exclusion no doubt takes its revenge in the Bene Gesserit command of Voice, and the male fear of it, a theme Herbert weaves contrapuntally throughout the six volumes of the series. The interplay of Bene Gesserit and Honored Matre uses of the Voice in trying to combat each other is truly fascinating to observe in these volumes, for it reveals the basic ideological positions of both societies with regard to discourses of power (*Chapterhouse,* 111). And the dialogue that Herbert takes up with women and women's voices (the women of the Bene Gesserit are represented as being in constant dialogue with the Others Within as well) seems an innovative twist on the feminist ideal of Sisterhood. Of course, whether or not the Dune series is ultimately feminist in the images and voices of women it projects is an open question. One thing seems certain, however, and that is that many strong independent women's voices can be heard in these last movements of Herbert's ecological fugue.

Chapter Seven
Critical Summary

Herbert's Other Fiction

Frank Herbert currently has nearly thirty books in print, twenty-three in the field of science fiction. His best-known works are part of what his publisher refers to as "the Dune cycle," or "the Dune Chronicles," though neither term is a very accurate description of how the series is organized as one long "ecological fugue." Any critical survey dealing with Herbert would necessarily have to deal with the nature and historical significance of these works primarily, for they have emerged as Herbert's major contribution to the field.

At present, the reputation of Herbert's other fiction is uncertain, though some works, such as *The Santaroga Barrier* and *Destination: Void,* have received critical readings that proclaim them accomplished efforts. *The Santaroga Barrier* (1968) is a utopian novel, unquestionably one of Herbert's most thought-provoking works. Unlike most of his other fiction, it takes place in modern America. The barrier referred to in the title is that set up by a prosperous farming community, Santaroga, in California, which is against all outsiders who want to exploit the valley commercially. Gilbert Dasein, a clinical psychologist with an old girlfriend in the community, accepts an assignment to do a "market survey" of Santaroga. Gradually, and only when it is too late and he himself is addicted, Dasein discovers that a hallucinogen called "jaspers" gives the Santarogans access to a communal mind. This communal mind, however, is deeply paranoid about outsiders, whom it considers "non-men," and has arranged for several fatal "accidents" to happen to other investigators before Dasein. Although Dasein confronts members of the community with this hidden violence, he has a hard time convincing them. The novel is marred by some static essay-type arguments between Dasein and Dr. Larry Piaget, the Santarogans' apologist, but argumentative passages such as these have long been the aesthetic problem of the utopian novel, which somehow has to provide an account of how the society got to be the way it is while at the same time involving the reader in an imaginative journey that makes the experience of living in that society vivid. Herbert accomplishes the latter by using Dasein's consciousness as his focalizer in the novel. All along as Dasein investigates the violence beneath the benign surface of the town, as he rekindles his love for his Santarogan girlfriend, Jenny, the reader is hoping that Dasein will help the Santarogans make an adjustment to reality by recognizing their death wishes toward outsiders, thereby making the community more healthy. Indeed we find much to admire among the conservative Santarogans, and accept some of their indictments of the outside world as a vicious sham. The real horror, comes, though, when Dasein himself arranges for an "accident" to happen to his boss who comes to visit him in hopes of finding out what has happened. When Dasein seems to absolve himself of responsibility for the accident at the inquest, we can no longer wholeheartedly accept the Santarogan way of life. The Santarogans, we realize, have lost their personal identities and have become masks for something sinister that is the same in all of them. We are chilled at the end to learn that the community has had plans for Dasein all along (Jenny had been a snare to tie him emotionally to the community), and that they are now planning to go on the offensive against the outside world with Dasein as their representative.

Herbert explored the territory of (supposedly) utopian societies in two other novels. *The Eyes of Heisenberg* (1966) depicts a civilization of the distant future and how it deals with the Heisenberg indeterminacy principle, which states that the observer is part of the experiment and is by no means a neutral observer. Every attempt to measure the subatomic realm expends energy and therefore alters the speed and location of elementary particles. Although this society claims to see indeterminately through the eyes of Heisenberg in its official policies, things have in fact rigidified into a hierarchical absolute system. The people of this civilization have found two ways of forestalling death. The dominant Optimen are genetically engineered individuals who are practically immortal because their enzymes are kept in perfect balance. They control the population and watch it unemotionally from seemingly Olympian heights. By contrast, the dominated Cyborgs achieve long life by replacing worn biological components with sophisticated prostheses. The Cyborgs are out to overthrow the Optimen with the help of an embryo resistant to the Optimen's contraceptive gas. The Durant embryo had become viable when subatomic particles caused a mutation in it during a fairly routine attempt at genetic engineering with a meson microscope. Thus have wild forces from outside this seemingly closed and static society reintroduced "the inelegant unexpectedness of naked Life," into it. The Cyborgs try to enlist the help of the Durants, but the parents are repelled by the tactics of both groups (the Cyborgs try to upset the delicate emotional natures of the Optimen by staging scenes of violence). They help create a conspiracy within a conspiracy to reestablish nature's way. Eventually a genetic surgeon named Svengaard finds a solution to the immediate problems of this society by coming up with the idea of implanting viable embryos in all Optimen—and all mere humans like the Durants—and retarding their development, thereby providing a natural means of balancing enzymes. This gets human evolution back on track (though it effectively ignores the Cyborgs), and fulfills a pattern of indeterminacy by reshaping the genetic environment so that the normal human life of people like the Durants will have some hope for the future. Herbert's point is that life cannot be totally maneuvered against the interests of living. Some critics find the mediation of the problem a bit contrived, and this criticism may be valid. The book does present, however, in an entertaining format ideas that are crucial to an understanding of Herbert as a philosophical thinker, ideas perhaps better realized aesthetically in an open-ended series. *The Eyes of Heisenberg* shows an absolute system closed in on itself disrupted by an outside force that introduces change and difference into the repetition of the same. Herbert was not a dialectical thinker—voices in a dialogue must remain unmerged—and we should not therefore expect to find entirely satisfactory solutions (i.e., absolutes) to the structural oppositions he sets up in his fictions. Herbert's continuing concern was to show the dangerous limits of all belief systems. This is as true of *The Eyes of Heisenberg* as it is of *Dune* that also deals with the nature of indeterminacy through the device of Paul's prescient visions.

Another "utopian" novel dealing with the outcome of human evolution is *Hellstrom's Hive* (1973). It focuses on the conflict between the Agency, a covert branch of the United States government, and the hive society of Nils Hellstrom. Hellstrom is known to the world as a man who has taken up the cause of ecology. Indeed, he is thought of as "some kind of ecological messiah." But Hellstrom's hive turns out to be a nightmare of cannibalism and torture for those who try to find out about the hive's true function—which is to preserve the human species. To Hellstrom, the hive is a cocoon from which the next stage in human evolution will emerge. To us, however, it evokes little more than horror and disgust. Yet none of the members of the Agency who investigate the hive have the dedication to an ideal that Hellstrom has. In fact, he is working toward a society in which he will have no place. After the hive swarms, hypersexual females will be queens of the hives. Since the Agency seems so unadmirable both in its heroes and its actions, some critics have argued that Herbert wants us to consider seriously Hellstrom's hive as a viable alternate to human society. But even Hellstrom's diaries, excerpts from which make up a good half of the novel and which are addressed to future readers to justify and explain, do little to humanize his project. Considering the fact that Herbert repeatedly warned against the dangers of fanaticism, and himself rejected "hot gospel" ecology, it seems likely that Hellstrom is a portrait of human ecology gone awry.

Destination: Void (1966), a novel about an attempt to create artificial consciousness, is admired as an example of what "cybernetic" science-fiction writing should be. An appendix to the revised edition even includes an explanation of the math relating to grid/field imbedment concepts employed by theorists of artificial intelligence who compare computer programming with certain human thought processes. The events in this novel are nearly all steps in the creation of the artificial consciousness, the "Ox," under crisis conditions aboard an enormous space colony ship whose computer has failed. It turns out that the failure was planned in order to drive the crew to accomplish this formidable task. The colonists, as well as the crew, are genetically engineered clones and are therefore considered expendable. The real theme of the book, as I read it, is the nature of cosmic consciousness, which each member of the crew assembling the Ox experiences momentarily in his or her own way. The book takes shape and interest as an intellectual debate about the nature of consciousness by characters who are themselves overtly Jungian personality types. In the course of this debate the notion of consciousness is subjected to an open-ended series of models—everything from existential phenomenology to gestalt psychology. The book's style is densely packed with the jargon of the science of artificial intelligence, yet to Herbert's credit not all the models are of Western origin. He also asks us to consider Zen ideas about what it really means to be awake. For the most part, though, the book is tied to Western assumptions and fears (quotes from Mary Shelley's *Frankenstein* open many of its sections) about the nature of artificial intelligence.

Herbert's first novel, *Under Pressure* (1956), is also admired for its science-fiction qualities, and for its realistic depiction of submarine technology, only slightly extrapolated from then-current knowledge and models. But the book has considerable interest also as a taut psychological thriller whose theme is that in an insane society a crazy man is normal. The book tells the story of a nuclear submarine crew on a dangerous mission to pirate undersea oil from an enemy base during a future war. Ensign John Ramsey, an undercover agent from the Bureau of Psychology, is sent on board *The Fenian Ram* to find out why so many missions and crews have been failing. To achieve his goal, Ramsey must become an integral member of the crew and the submarine's enveloped world with its own special ecology (one of the earliest uses of the word *ecology* in a science-fiction novel occurs in *Under Pressure,* if not, in fact, the first). Through a series of crises, the last of which forces him into catatonic shock, Ramsey discovers that the crews are suffering from an unconscious anticipation of birth trauma. He comes to see and feel the submarine as a kind of perambulating womb looking for a place to spew out its crew. Furthermore, the entire experience causes Ramsey to revise his belief in psychology as a supposedly objective science of mind. He realizes that there is one kind of sanity on the surface and another in the submarines. Commander Sparrow of *The Fenian Ram* may appear schizoid to the clinical mind, but he has adapted to the insane world of his submarine rather well in his quest for security, making himself literally part of it. Ramsey gains a critical perspective on his discipline and concludes that he will have to resist the tendency of psychoanalysts to offer their systems as substitutes for religion while setting themselves up as messiahs.

Most of Herbert's other novels, when discussed or reviewed by critics at all, are considered "good yarns," without literary merit because in them ideas seem to be of greater significance than character or plot. From the point of view of mainstream literary criticism, this lack of characterization is thought to be a flaw. Yet one has to consider the demands of the audience and the facts of publication as well. Many of these novels had their start as short stories in science-fiction magazines which were not known for publishing works of high literary quality (see chronology), but which did maintain standards of excellence within their own field. The problem of how to read the science-fiction novel on its own terms as having its own poetics and values remains. I can only offer a terse critical account of the remainder of Herbert's novels here and offer in some cases suggestions about how they might profitably be read.

Although ecological thinking is a concern in almost all of Herbert's novels, *The Green Brain* (1966) is the novel that focuses most directly and most single-mindedly on the themes of ecological destruction. The novel is set in the twenty-first century in Brazil when population pressures and advancing technology have encouraged the Third World to make total war on the earth's insect populations. Unknown to other countries, the Chinese have succeeded in their country in destroying all insects dangerous to man, but China is rapidly becoming a wasteland. The insects respond in the Matto Grosso by massing together and creating a superconscious "Green Brain" to communicate with the human race and warn it of the impending sterilization of the planet. As a character, the Green Brain is little more than a mouthpiece for Herbert's ecological ideas. As such, it delivers several lectures about the nature of "greenhouse Earth" and the interdependence of life on our planet. But then this is as it should be, for the burden of proof has fallen on the insects because the humans are mainly concerned with saving face and not lives. Herbert does give the novel some interesting twists. What could have been the horror of insect domination (human simulacra and body parts constructed out of insects provide some effective "insect fear" passages) turns out to be a healthy, positive step. The insects are prepared to give mankind "the greatest gift in the universe," the sense of living Time.

The Heaven Makers (1968) takes a paranoid theme and makes it into a commentary on the nature and function of storytelling. What if most of human history were the creation of a superior and immortal alien race, invisible to us, that has been directing it for their own entertainment purposes? In *The Heaven Makers* this thesis is literally true. Humans are regarded by the immortal and bored Chem as an endless pot of self-generating stories. The reader interested in exploring Herbert's ideas about the paradoxical nature of fiction—it seems to be necessary for us to cognitively understand our world—should read this book closely. Among the paradoxes the book explores is the nature of the finite and the infinite in storytelling. Human stories provide entertainment for the Chem who are bored because their futures are unimportant. Human stories save them from the "fatality" of boredom. Yet, Herbert makes clear, the Chem are locked into a closed system of communication, and therefore cannot grasp the real truth about the infinite universe. Ironically it is a melodramatic story of an insane creature who slays his mate that introduces the dangerous outside into the seemingly closed system of Chem communal life.

Herbert's last novel, a collaboration with his son Brian, also combines the themes of science fiction with a reflection on the nature of storytelling. The basic premise of *Man of Two Worlds* (1986) is that all of Earth—indeed all of the universe—is the creation of the fertile imagination of an alien world, Dreenor. The Dreens are storytellers with an infinite capacity to "idmage" new planets as creative stories. Earth is the product of a Great Story because its inhabitants are possessed of free will. The Dreens have been observing Earth for a long time and are concerned about what might happen if Earth ever finds out about their activities. The plot concerns what happens when the mind of an Earthman (the heir to a newspaper empire and hence a storyteller himself) is accidentally fused with that of a Dreen. *Man of Two Worlds* is obviously a send-up of many science-fiction themes—creator figures and races, their responsibilities, and the chance that humankind may be a casual toy.

Whipping Star (1970) is also a lighthearted romp, this time through the subgenre of detective-science fiction. In this novel an agent from the galactic Bureau of Sabotage named Jorj X. McKie has to solve the mystery of communicating with strange alien beings known as Calabans, who turn out to be living stars. One of them has been trapped into a seemingly unbreakable contract that will destroy the known universe if it continues. It is being whipped by a psychotic sadomasochist who derives gratification from debasing aliens. The Calaban's energy is weakening and with it the very fabric of reality. With a combination of legal and communicative skills, McKie succeeds in freeing the Calaban, who falls in love with him, and saves the universe.

In the sequel to this novel, *The Dosadi Experiment* (1977), the Bureau of Sabotage is still dedicated to eradicating the old imprints in the galactic ConSentiency, "the old futile seeking after absolutes of sameness." Through his adroit actions McKie finds a loophole in another dangerous Calaban contract, this time binding a star to form a "Godwall" around a secret body-trade planet that is a bid for immortality on the part of a cabal within the ConSentiency made up of humans and froglike Gowachin. The tone of this sequel is much more serious, however, being in fact a satire on legalism. In order to expose the cabal, McKie has to become a Gowachin lawyer and deal with the intricacies of an alien legal system. The basic Gowachin attitude toward their law is "respectful disrespect." They are a people whose most consummate pleasure comes when the currents of their own laws are changed artistically. McKie's activities in the Gowachin court arena deftly convict the guilty and integrate an alien legal discourse into the existing framework of the Bureau of Sabotage. Because of these legal maneuverings—Herbert invents a new loophole in Gowachin law each time McKie seems trapped—*The Dosadi Experiment* is a fiction that seems constituted out of loopholes in its own narrative structure.

The Godmakers (1972) of the title are a religious order located on the planet Amal who have learned to use the energies present in religion ("psi focus") to create gods. By means of prophetic visions they select candidates for such a process. Through a series of god-ordeals and tests, Lewis Orne gains insight and knowledge into his powers. However, Orne does not become a rogue god demanding that humans learn how to worship him, as the computer does in *Destination: Void.* Lewis Orne confronts an infinite universe and tells the Abbod who summoned him to Amal that "the faith we have is the faith we create," almost the exact words of Leto II in *Children of Dune* who tells his father Paul that he has no faith other than what he creates. The Abbod warns Orne about humankind's dangerous attraction to absolutes, especially in its gods. Orne vanishes from Amal a god, but the novel ends with him treating his own powers with wry amusement; on his tomb he wants inscribed the words "He chose infinity one step at a time." Orne chooses to play out the role of an adventure hero, honeymooning his sweetheart and promising humankind "an open account in the bank of Time." Anything can still happen.

Soul Catcher (1972) is about a crazed Indian who wants to throw off the world of the white man that has raped his sister and driven her to suicide. Instructed by the spirit world, he captures a thirteen-year-old white boy (Hoquat in his language), drags him through the wilds of a national forest for two weeks, and then kills him in a sacrificial ceremony in which he hopes to win back his lost Indian soul. By this act he hopes also to send a powerful message of retribution back to the white community.

Soul Catcher is Herbert's only attempt at the realistic novel. Herbert had Indian friends as a boy, and the book seems well enough researched as far as Indian rituals and beliefs go. It conveys a feeling for the Indian view of violence and transgression and has some moments of genuine psychological insight into hostages and the people who take them. It cannot, however, compete in emotional impact, with other novels in the genre, such as Dee Brown's *Bury My Heart at Wounded Knee.* Still, the book is a sensitive and disturbing plea for understanding of our native peoples and their problems, if not an overt statement of "red power."

The White Plague (1982) is also a tale of a man driven insane by the loss of loved ones. A molecular biologist visiting Dublin loses his wife and twin sons when a terrorist bomb explodes on a crowded street corner. This shattering sense of loss drives O'Neill into madness, but it also drives him into a genius mode by giving him access to another personality capable of using O'Neill's knowledge to create a plague that will exact his revenge. Through recombinant DNA techniques, O'Neill fashions a disease that kills only women. Much of the action in the novel depicts the problems that beset the various scientific teams that assemble to handle the crisis and O'Neill's trek across a nightmarish Ireland to witness the results of his white plague. This novel is truly science fiction, for it shows in detail how the narrative world is altered irrevocably by O'Neill's innovative techniques with DNA. Surprisingly though, the novel ends with optimism because the discoveries in genetics made by the research teams may far outweigh the effect of the plague once society returns to safe population levels. The teams realize that since they have found a cure for the plague in tracing O'Neill's steps, other diseases may be erased as well. A black shadow can now be lifted from mankind's future.

Herbert coauthored two sequels to *Destination: Void* with the West Coast poet, Bill Ransom. Both *The Jesus Incident* (1979) and *The Lazarus Effect* (1983) deal with themes dear to Herbert. The former is an exploration of religious games and the theology of play, a book in which Christmas and aquaculture are united in the ultimate act of evolution: worship. *The Lazarus Effect* explores the nature of what it means to be human by interrogating the discourses of two mutated societies that try to define "the normal" in relation to each other. In both books, as in *The White Plague,* out of seeming chaos and madness in which Pandora's box is opened come new possibilities for humankind's future.

Herbert's short stories are on the whole too unremarkable for there to be adequate reason to provide an account of them here. One story, however, first published in 1973 and reprinted in *Eye,* is to my mind the finest embodiment of the mature Herbert's philosophical ideas outside of the Dune series. "Death of a City" is a scintillating fable of the far future that proclaims the need for constant intellectual struggle against all "lethal absolutes," while at the same time indicating the necessity of finding and affirming the *differences* of life instead of the repetition of the same. The plot involves a City Doctor whose task it is to diagnose why the most beautiful city ever conceived and built by man is now subject to violence and vandalism and a declining population. In this city every expectation of the human senses had been met, but it is in this very conformity to human demands that the cancerous flaw arose. The Doctor discovers that there is nothing in this city any longer to make the species "face up to Infinity." Herbert may set up dichotomies in a story—here the ugly and the beautiful—but their essential tension must never be resolved. He was a resolutely antidialectical thinker.

Herbert's Reputation

Dune (1965), which won the Nebula Award that year and the Hugo Award the following year, is considered one of the most popular science-fiction novels of the last twenty years. Indeed, in a poll conducted by the news magazine of the science-fiction community, *Locus* (15 April 1975), Herbert's *Dune* was voted the all-time best science-fiction novel.[1] In the academic sphere *Dune* is frequently taught in science-fiction courses. The most adequate guide to the canon that is constituted by science-fiction teaching today, compiled by Jack Williamson and published in the *CEA Critic* (November 1974), lists *Dune* as one of the most popular books used in introductions to the subject.[2] In terms of the general reading public, *Dune*'s success over the years has been enormous and significant. It has sold over ten million copies in numerous editions. When Herbert completed the third book of the series, *Children of Dune* (1976), it became an authentic hardcover best-seller with seventy-five thousand copies sold (not including book club sales).[3] It was the first hardcover best-seller ever in the science fiction field. As other books in the series appeared, they were reviewed in major critical organs such as the *New York Times Book Review.*[4] It is something of a tribute to Herbert's success on college campuses that the *National Lampoon* wrote a parody of *Dune* in 1984 (the only other book to have been so honored is Tolkien's *Lord of the Rings*).[5]

Given the size of this readership, both within and without the academic community, and the fact of Herbert's enormous popularity, it is surprising to learn than he has received very little critical attention. He has never been the subject of a volume of selected critical essays or even a bibliography. Only three studies examine his work at any length. L. David Allen's long essay in the Cliffs Notes Series (1975) argues convincingly for the unity and continuity of *Dune* and *Dune Messiah,* though readers in the science-fiction community thought the latter book did not live up to the expectations created by *Dune* with regard to the hero. By looking at the two novels as a sophisticated form of heroic romance, Allen is able to show that this archetypal pattern makes the apotheosis of the hero in *Dune Messiah* natural and inevitable. This study is, however, now outdated because of the publication of *Children of Dune* a year later, in which Herbert delivers extensive revisions in the heroic pattern he had established with the first two volumes. David M. Miller's 1980 monograph argues that the novels of Frank Herbert form a unified treatment of the problem of achieving a "dynamic homeostasis," between order and disorder.[6] This is certainly a valid insight into Herbert's themes, for it recognizes implicitly the idea of infinity in Herbert's fiction. The theme of dynamic homeostasis can have no end. This study is good at pointing out that Herbert's themes make for unsatisfactory endings because there can be no end to the dynamic tension between "flow-permanence." However, focused as it is on the form of the content in Herbert's novels, it does not examine Herbert's relationship to his audience.

In *Frank Herbert* (1981) Timothy O'Reilly traces the reception of the *Dune* trilogy among readers and critics of science fiction, noting in particular the influence that John W. Campbell, in his function of editor of *Analog,* had on the development of the series.[7] Campbell, while praising *Dune* as a true heroic saga in which the hero overcomes his enemies and triumphs against fate, stated his objections to publishing *Dune Messiah* in a letter to Herbert, which is now in the archives at Fullerton. The correspondence between Herbert and Campbell could help us to objectify what theorists of reception call "the horizon of expectations" in a particular community of readers, that is, the intersubjective structure of expectations which registers literary deviations and modifications with exaggerated sensitivity, in this case the demands of "science-fictioneers," so-called by Campbell in his response to *Dune Messiah.*[8] In this book Campbell found only an antihero who is the helpless pawn of fate, whereas he knew his readers demanded "stories of strong men who exert themselves, inspire others, and make a monkey's uncle out of the malign fates."[9] On the surface *Dune* may have appeared to be very much in the Campbell mode, but *Dune Messiah* is definitely a move out of the norms of "Golden Age" science fiction. Campbell was also something of a boy scout in sexual matters, which leads one to believe that the explicit use of sex in later volumes in the Dune series would not have met with his approval either.

At any rate, O'Reilly notes that among the "science-fictioneers" of the sort Campbell himself perhaps best exemplifies, the reaction to the books coming after *Dune* (O'Reilly only discusses the trilogy) was often puzzled anger. They wondered what happened to change Herbert's views so much. They were puzzled especially by *Children of Dune,* in which the heroic ideal is seriously undermined. Why did Herbert turn from presenting one of the most admirable heroes in modern science fiction, Paul Atreides, to a massive preoccupation with his son, the God Emperor of Dune, Leto II? O'Reilly answers this question with an intriguing analysis showing in fact that the two sequels are an integral part of a design Herbert had on his readers from the outset. According to O'Reilly, who interviewed Herbert on his intentions (and it seems clear from the full transcript of the interview in the archives at Fullerton that O'Reilly himself was one of those puzzled readers), the Dune trilogy was very carefully constructed to build up Paul as a hero in the reader's eyes so that his failure in *Dune Messiah* would reach across with full intensity to teach him a lesson in the dangers of hero worship—what Herbert referred to elsewhere as "the superhero syndrome," that tendency in human societies to look for an ideal person, projected from the Jungian collective unconscious, to solve all our problems.

This thesis (that the Dune trilogy was designed to make the reader aware of his own participation in the heroic ideal) is O'Reilly's main contribution to Herbert studies. It seems to me to be confirmed beyond a doubt by the evidence he presents. However, in the closing pages of his book he asks what to my mind is an interesting question to which he gives only a simplistic answer. The question is why this underlying unity is not more apparent from the outset. What is it about *Dune,* and ourselves as readers, O'Reilly asks, that makes it hard to see the unified purpose of the trilogy, so apparent once it has been pointed out? O'Reilly's answer is that, while there are clues about the negative aspects of Paul's messianic efforts discoverable by the discerning reader, we are too busy cheering Paul's actions to notice that his success is only apparent. The pleasures of our identification with Paul hide the negations of the text. We are blinded by our own submission to the hero mystique. It seems to me that the kind of escapist identification O'Reilly assumes can and does certainly occur, but only among those who are reading *Dune* for its entertainment value alone. Actually, as I have tried to show in chapter 2, I think complete identification with Paul is difficult due to the underlying system of indeterminacies in the text, which introduce negations into our image of Paul at crucial points.

One concept that emerges from O'Reilly's study, although he is not interested in academic notions of literary history such as the "horizon of expectations" mentioned above, is that the *Dune* series is clearly a departure from the kind of science fiction written during the so-called Golden Age when the norm was extrapolation from the hard sciences (although he in fact promoted L. Ron Hubbard's ideas, Campbell argued that sociology, psychology, and parapsychology were not true sciences, not yet anyway). This idea is taken up by two other critics, John L. Grigsby and Brian Aldiss.

In an article published in *Science Fiction Studies* (later amplified in another article a few years later) Grigsby compares and contrasts Herbert's Dune trilogy with Asimov's earlier *Foundation* series, the idea of which Campbell suggested to Asimov.[10] He finds that Herbert's trilogy is an ironic reversal and parody of Asimov's series, where psychohistorians control minds, blot out memories, and erase thoughts to keep "normal" humans from developing in the "wrong" way or from discovering that Hari Seldon's psychohistorians (it should be mentioned that "psychohistory" is not psychology, but a statistical science that predicts the behavior of human societies) exist, and where the unbelievable assumption is that such demeaning acts are the best course for mankind, since they avoid a longer period of barbarism. In *Children of Dune* Grigsby finds Herbert reversing this situation in his ending, which allows us to perceive the planned universe and its controllers from the point of view of its products—Leto and Ghanima. Leto sees ultimate horror in his visions, horror which leads to revolt sooner or later or a return to a sort of necessary barbarism. Grigsby finds many points of comparison between the two series, labeling Asimov a scientist and Herbert a romanticist-philosopher. The main point, though, is that Herbert's complexity of vision led him to parody Asimov and thereby, I would say, to go beyond the somewhat narrow (from Herbert's point of view anyway) expectations of science fiction of the Golden Age.

But while Asimov's *Foundation* series and Herbert's *Dune* series have been compared on the basis of their different views about rational planning for the future, what has not been sufficiently understood is how great a difference exists in their views about the nature of language. Each writer in fact holds a view of language that is the exact opposite of the other. To Asimov (at least in the *Foundation* series), language can be "disambiguated" by the use of symbolic logic, an idea suggested to him by John W. Campbell, but which he nonetheless worked into the structure of the series. Here it appears that language can be stripped of all its qualifying statements, its evasions and "loopholes," to provide a rational and scientific basis for understanding (see especially *Foundation,* "The Encyclopedists," section 5). Furthermore, this view of language is reflected in Asimov's plain style in which the emphasis is on communication. For Herbert on the contrary we can never get behind language to frame such an objective account of how language communicates because we are always already immersed in it as a social practice. And the "loopholes" and paradoxes of language which Asimov distrusts are the very means by which Herbert constructed his most intriguing character, Leto II, the God Emperor of Dune, as indicated in chapter 5. This contrast, more than anything else, demonstrates that Asimov is typical of the optimistic and naive linguistic views of the Campbell era in American science fiction with its belief in unclouded reason dominating the play of language, and that Herbert is a transitional figure pointing toward a more "decentered" view of language as a field in which the speaker is both dominated and dominating at the same time.

Brian Aldiss had discussed Herbert before in his history of science fiction, *Billion Year Spree,* arguing that although Campbellian science fiction is present in *Dune,* so, too, is an attention to sensuous detail, which is the antithesis of Campbell who was concerned mainly with science fiction as a vehicle for ideas.[11] In a recent keynote address he amplified these ideas and was much more specific about his scheme for the periodization of science fiction and *Dune*'s role as a transitional work. For Aldiss *Dune* represents both the culmination of Campbellian thought and the emergence of the modern period in science fiction: "Most of its subject matter had been deployed in *Astounding* [the science-fiction magazine Campbell edited] for some years. Certainly desert planets were no new thing, nor galactic empires, nor skulduggery, nor heroic leaders, nor telepathic powers, nor even weird women. What was new was the emphasis on the formative power that Arrakis held over its human societies. That was new, as was the scale of the enterprise, though we did not realize that in 1965. And, because of that scale, the process we were to witness was also new."[12]

The Dune series is gaining stature among historians of the science-fiction novel. I have tried to give a sense of the process of development of Herbert's "ecological fugue" in this study. My hope is that someday the Dune novels will be ranked among the best of all American novels—not just science-fiction ones. Meanwhile, and until that time comes, the reader who wants to gain a sense of the scale of Herbert's achievement by reading detailed essays describing the society, history, and characters of the novels up to and including *God Emperor of Dune* should consult Willis McNelly's *The Dune Encyclopedia* (1984). Although Herbert was not officially involved in the project, which in many instances is deadpan serious while spoofing certain aspects of Herbert's world, he did give it his approval and wanted to know what the encyclopedia had to say about the Scattering and Famine times so that he could plan further volumes in the series. What is more, Herbert read large portions of *God Emperor of Dune,* then in the final stages, to McNelly during the compiling of the volume so that McNelly could keep abreast of developments.

What resulted from all this scholarly activity—forty-three people were involved in writing entries—is something that would have delighted Jorge Luis Borges: a real encyclopedia of an imaginary world, complete with a maze of ramifying footnotes and bibliographies of *every* book, magazine, manuscript, or ridulian crystal that the authors "used" in preparing their entries. It provides useful chronologies, but goes far further than simply serving as a factual guide to a fictional world. Some of the articles are querulous, taking issue with other imaginary antagonists about the nature of events and people in the Dune series; others are scholarly; others objective; and many entertaining in the very best sense of the word. The contributors even created characters not in the Dune series, including the Imperium's Shakespeare, Harq al-Harba, for whose life and works they provide a brief analysis. The encyclopedia is so internally consistent that it even provides short discussions about whether or not Leto II or Harq al-Ada (Farad'n of *Children of Dune*) might have written some of al-Harba's plays. Because it does have this dimension of intertextuality, and because it "criticizes" the *Dune* series in a dialogical way (one entry speculates that the Reverend Mother Gaius Helen Mohiam was the mother of Jessica, instead of the woman mentioned by Herbert) by adding more voices to its great conversation, *The Dune Encyclopedia* is an entirely appropriate extention of Herbert's compositional methods and his imaginative world at the hands of others.

Notes and References

Chapter One

1. Ben Bova, "Frank Herbert," *Science Fiction Chronicle,* April 1986, 24.

2. Transcript of interview with Herbert on 27 February 1978, by Timothy O'Reilly, in the archives at California State University, Fullerton (CSF), 11. Also on the same page: "I call it [conversation], a dance too. . . . It really is a jazz performance. There is no other conversation in the universe that has ever been quite like the one we're having now. And there never will be another one quite like it."

3. "Listening to the Left Hand," in *The Book of Frank Herbert* (New York: Berkley Books, 1981), 215. This article, which originally appeared in *Harper's Magazine* (December 1973), is probably the clearest presentation of Herbert's ideas about language and its influence on thought as well as the tendency of the human intellect to demand fixed, absolute meanings from an infinite universe of relativity and change.

4. The phrase is taken from Fred Pohl's eulogy for Herbert, *Science Fiction Chronicle,* April 1986, 26.

5. Taped interview with Herbert, 1 August 1980, by Robert Wright, in archives at CSF.

6. O'Reilly interview, 8.

7. Ben Reuven, "The Dunes Sayer: Turning a Prophet," *Los Angeles Times,* 25 April 1976, 3.

8. Anecdote supplied by Professor McNelly in personal correspondence.

9. Willis E. McNelly, "In Memoriam: Frank Herbert," *Bulletin of the Science Fiction Writers of America,* Spring 1986, 24.

10. David Michael Ettlin, "A Great Imagination Stilled," *Cleveland Plain Dealer,* 16 February 1986, 20.

11. This study assumes that the primary condition of all discourse is social. Within and across countries, discourses differ in terms of their "speech genre," their own typical forms of utterance. Discourses differ also with the kinds of institutions and social practices in which they take shape, and with the positions of those who speak and those whom they address. Literature, with its genres and conventions, is also a form of social discourse, but one in which other discourses are represented or reported. According to M. M. Bakhtin, the fundamental object, specific to the novel as a genre, and the one that gives it stylistic originality, is *man speaking* and his *discourse.* It is not the image

of man himself that is characteristic of the genre of the novel, but the image of language. Furthermore, "the novel always includes in itself the activity of coming to know another's word, a coming to knowledge whose process is represented in the novel" (M. M. Bakhtin, *The Dialogical Imagination,* Michael Holquist trans. and ed. [Austin: University of Texas Press, 1981], 353). I am assuming that Herbert's career as a journalist made him familiar with a broad range of social discourses, from the "city desk" of a newspaper, to political speechwriting, to the conversations one might hear at a science-fiction convention between fans and authors. In the *Dune* series social groups will have their own languages: the Fremen, the Bene Gesserit, the aristocratic Atreides, etc., which gives the series its mixture of styles. The hero, say, Paul Atreides in *Dune,* has to find his way through the language of these social groups just as we do.

12. Jane Hipolito and Willis E. McNelly, eds., *Mars, We Love You* (New York: Pyramid Books, 1973), 315.

13. Untranscribed Wright interview.

14. Anecdote supplied by Professor McNelly in personal correspondence.

15. Wright interview.

16. Ibid.

17. Ross Stagner, "Frank Herbert, Master of Dune," *Psychology Today,* October 1984, 72.

18. "Frank Herbert," in *Science Fiction Writers,* ed. E. F. Bleiler (New York: Charles Scribner's Sons, 1982), 380.

Chapter Two

1. "Dune Genesis," *Omni,* July 1980, 74. The origin and development of the *Dune* series is also discussed in a taped interview with Frank Herbert, conducted by Willis McNelly, 3 February 1969, transcription in the archives at CSF. I have drawn primarily on these two sources for my own account.

2. For an ecological account of reader response, see Louise Rosenblatt, *The Reader, The Text, The Poem* (Carbondale: Southern Illinois University Press, 1978), 18. For an account of "ecological semantics," see Katerina Clark and Michael Holquist, *Mikhail Bakhtin* (Cambridge: Harvard University Press, 1984), 227, and *Dune* [302/307] where Paul takes the name *Muad'Dib,* or "Desert Mouse."

3. L. David Allen, *Dune and Other Works* (Lincoln, Nebr.: Cliffs Notes, 1975), 28–35.

4. Mikhail Bakhtin, *Problems of Dostoevsky's Poetics,* Theory and History of Literature Series, vol. 8, Caryl Emerson, ed. and trans., introduction by Wayne Booth (Minneapolis: University of Minnesota Press, 1984), 104.

5. For further discussion, see V. N. Volosinov, *Marxism and the Philosophy of Language,* trans. Ladislav Matejka and I. R. Titunik (Cambridge: Harvard University Press, 1986), 141–59.

6. For further discussion of the formal and grammatical aspects of these three modes, see Dorrit Cohn, *Transparent Minds* (Princeton: Princeton University Press, 1978). Cohn terms the three modes of psycho-narration, quoted monologue, and narrated monologue. In *Problems* Bakhtin shows how Dostoevsky's monologues are generally structured as "micro-dialogs," flooded with the inner speech and words of others (74–75). It would be easy to show that many monologues in *Dune* have these properties too. Beginning with *Children of Dune,* the Other Memories of characters are also represented overtly as dialogues. Thus Leto and Ghanima converse with their dead mother and father, still alive in a kind of psychic Hades. Or rather, they allow themselves to be possessed by them.

7. *Dune* (New York: Chilton Books, 1965), 128; hereafter page numbers cited in parentheses in the text. The second set of numbers in such citations are the corresponding pages in the paperback edition, in this case, 130–31. Herbert's several drafts of this scene show considerable variation in what he intended to have put in italics and quotation marks, which would seem to indicate that he was quite aware of the problems involved in reported speech. In the setting copy, for example, the phrases "shortening of the way" and "Kwisatz Haderach" are also in italics, making it clear that they are in Jessica's mind. Also in the setting copy, Jessica once again reacts internally to Kynes's ominous words, this time uttered to Bewt, about the nature of change. Jessica hears them as speaking "right out of the Panoplia Propheticus." In the published version Kynes only reacts physically to Bewt's words. Perhaps Herbert felt that too much layering would complicate the scene. In any case the passage is redundant, for Jessica's reaction to Kynes's words has already been established.

8. I am thankful to Willis McNelly for suggesting to me in a letter that this scene reads like a one-act play; I have tried to analyze it in terms of its "experienced speech" patterns as such. Herbert's own reading of the scene can be found on Caedmon Records. The quote about the reader's participation is taken from the liner notes to *Dune: The Banquet Scene,* 1977.

9. Volosinov, "Exposition of the Problem of Reported Speech," in *Marxism,* 115–23. This authorship of this text is sometimes attributed to Bakhtin.

10. John G. Cawelti, *Adventure, Mystery, Romance* (Chicago: Chicago University Press, 1976), 17–19.

11. Wolfgang Iser, *The Act of Reading* (Baltimore: Johns Hopkins University Press, 1978), 186–87.

12. Bakhtin, "Epic and Novel," in *The Dialogical Imagination,* 31.

Chapter Three

1. *Dune Messiah* 11/11; hereafter page references cited in parentheses in the text.

2. In Herbert's handwriting on a xerox of the Bronso of Ix death-cell interview, which Herbert added to the paperback version at the suggestion of his editor. In CSF archives.

3. For an account of internally persuasive discourse and its role in the ideological shaping of the self, see Bakhtin, *The Dialogical Imagination,* 342ff.

Chapter Four

1. *Dune Messiah,* 201/233.

2. *Children of Dune* (New York: Putnam's, 1976), 275/269; hereafter page references cited in parentheses in the text.

3. *God Emperor of Dune* (New York: Putnam's, 1981), 406/418.

4. Tape #15/3 in the archives at CSF, in which Professor McNelly and Herbert discuss the definitions and background meanings of the people, places, and elements contained in the *Dune* series.

Chapter Five

1. *God Emperor of Dune* (New York: Putnam's, 1981), 49/41; hereafter page references cited in parentheses in the text.

2. Herbert's handwritten notes, in a box labeled "First Draft II of *God Emperor of Dune*" at CSF, give a clearer picture of this threat from Ix:

A real physical threat from combined forces of Ix and Tleilax . . . Ixians have developed a Taylor complexity amplifier (CA) which approaches chaos. Secret cells in both Ixian and Tleilaxu societies control the conspiracy. Hwi Noree is not a part of the conspiracy but is considered a weapon by the Ixians. Great rolling waves of near-chaos originate with the Tleilaxu and Ixians screening some sort of action. This causes Leto to make frequent checks on the course of the Golden Path (which lay in at earliest - Ch. II). Golden Path continues but the observers cannot tell if he [Leto] is present personally or is merely recording events which *still* are to be. . . . Conspiracy aims to drive Leto into final metamorphosis at earliest possible moment, then grab control of the Empire. Hwi is the key to this . . . by forcing Leto to grab at remnants of his lost humanity, thus precipitating hormonal imbalances which his new body will suppress.

3. In the first draft of the *God Emperor,* at CSF, Siona tells Duncan that *arafel* means "the cloud darkness out of which the ten commandments were uttered," and indeed *arafel* is the regular biblical Hebrew word for "cloud," used in the book of Exodus. By saying that the Ixians cannot create *arafel,* he may mean just the capacity to hide from predators, as God hides in the dark cloud on Mount Sinai. But the idea of a commanding voice is also present here, as is the power of Infinity. Darwi Odrade, a distant descendant of Siona

and a Bene Gesserit, finds part of Leto's spice hoard in *Heretics of Dune*; it has been hidden from predators for millennia. The key to finding the hoard is the word *arafel* etched in stone, and inside on the walls of the sietch are written Leto's commandments to the latter-day Bene Gesserit. He even predicts that a Bene Gesserit sister will one day read his words, probably because only the Sisterhood will at that time have any knowledge of the language in which he writes. This is a good example of how Herbert deliberately created secrets in the narrative, which resist our easy and orderly comprehension of it, introducing a measure of chaos into it. See discussion in chapter 6.

4. Also in the first draft is the following passage left out of the published version:

You will marvel that sometimes I use the first person, sometimes the second or third. It is all the same to me because I am the woven thread of these pasts. I trust that in your search for truth you will recognize the changes and make your own connections. I am confident that you will do this in the name of trying to understand me, to "take me in." You will not understand me, of course. The harder you try the more remote I will become until finally I will vanish, the Living God become ethereal myth.

Chapter Six

1. *Heretics of Dune* (New York: Putnam's, 1984), 27/19; hereafter page references cited in parentheses in the text.

2. For an account of how techniques of power have operated on the discourse of sexuality, see Michel Foucault, *The History of Sexuality,* vol. 1, Robert Hurley trans. (New York: Vintage Books, 1980).

3. Herbert's notes reveal that he originally intended the Tleilaxu (at Bene Gesserit command) to give this ghola the "Siona-screen." There is some debate in the book about whether Duncan has the screen or not because some of his ancestors were descendants of Siona. Just to be on the safe side, the Sisterhood decides to keep him imprisoned in the no-ship on Chapterhouse as the novel ends. Probably Herbert rejected the idea because, had he used it, there would have been less motivation for Duncan to stay in the no-ship, and the earlier Harkonnen no-globe.

4. Herbert's notes reveal that he intended Teg's agony to simulate the Reverend Mother experience with the Spice Agony, called s'tori (*satori*—a Japanese term meaning the understanding of the truth of Zen). Herbert originally conceived Teg's experience as a kind of enlightenment, his being more fully awake after the experience, and also envisioned Teg's anguish that he had not achieved this earlier: "All of those years at a level where life mostly flickered and never flamed high!"

5. Herbert never employed the idea in *Heretics,* but his notes indicate that one twist in the plot was to have been that the Bene Gesserit would have

worked out accords with the Lost Ones to find out whether they had encountered planets that would be sure to match Rakis sufficiently for worms and sandtrout to propagate—another threat to the Tleilaxu, Ix, and the Guild.

6. *Chapterhouse: Dune* (New York: Putnam's, 1985), 53; hereafter page references cited in parentheses in the text.

Chapter Seven

1. As reported by Mike Ashley, *The Illustrated Book of Science Fiction Lists* (New York: Cornerstone Library, 1982), 19. This poll was recently retaken. *Dune* won again, with an even more commanding lead than in 1975. *Locus* Vol. 20, No. 8 (August 1982), 32.

2. Jack Williamson, "SF in the Classroom," in *Science Fiction: The Academic Awakening*, ed. Willis McNelly, supplement to *CEA Critic* 37, 1 (November 1974): 12.

3. For an account of *Dune*'s publishing history, see David Hartwell, *Age of Wonders* (New York: Walker & Co., 1984), 31–33.

4. Gerald Jonas, "The Sandworm Saga," *New York Times Book Review*, 17 May 1981, 15, 28.

5. Ellis Weiner, *Doon* (New York: Pocket Books, 1984). This book is a hilarious parody of Herbert's style and ideas. Doon is a "dessert planet," a sugar-covered wasteland patrolled by a terrifying species of giant pretzel. Picking up on Herbert's ideas about improvisation, the parodist calls Jessica "Jazzica." But most of the parody derives from treating *Dune* as "culinary art" (see below) and from jokes made on our society's food and advertising industries. The book is probably a good antidote to the filmed version of *Dune*, which appeared also in 1984, riding on a wave of high-pressure advertising that spawned everything from bubble gum cards to plastic sandworms, action figure toys, and comic books. Herbert's own negative comments about the financial backers of the film, who are probably the ones ultimately responsible for the film's appearance in such a badly edited version, can be found in the introduction to *Eye*.

6. David M. Miller, *Frank Herbert*, Starmont Reader's Guides (Mercer Island, Wash.: Starmont House, 1980), 9.

7. Timothy O'Reilly, *Frank Herbert*, Recognitions Series (New York: Frederick Ungar, 1981), 152–54.

8. For an account of the horizonal structure of expectations (*Erwartungshorizont*) and its ability to be objectified by means of a hermeneutics of question and answer, see Hans Robert Jauss, *Towards an Aesthetic of Reception*, Timothy Bahti, trans., Theory and History of Literature, vol. 2 (Minneapolis: University of Minnesota Press, 1980). Jauss's aesthetics of reception distinguishes between certain works whose negativity demands a horizonal change on the part of the reader and "culinary art"—enjoyable popular literature—on the other. In chapter 2 of this study I have presented my views on

the negativity that can be found in *Dune* by the discerning reader. Actually, *Dune* is good entertainment, and I am certainly not disparaging those who simply want to read it on that level.

9. As quoted in O'Reilly, *Herbert*, 188.

10. John L. Grigsby, "Asimov's 'Foundation' Trilogy and Herbert's 'Dune' Trilogy: A Vision Reversed," *Science Fiction Studies* 8, no. 24 (July, 1981):149–55.

11. Brian W. Aldiss, *Billion Year Spree* (New York: Shocken Books, 1974), 274–76. The second, expanded edition of this book, *Trillion Year Spree*, gives a lively account of all the Dune books, and contrasts Herbert's willingness to change as writer with other "dinosaurs" of the Golden Age who did not (Asimov, Van Vogt, Hubbard).

12. "What Should an SF Novel Be About?" *Fantasy Review* 9, no. 4 (April 1986):6.

Selected Bibliography

PRIMARY SOURCES

A. Fiction

The Book of Frank Herbert. New York: Daw Books, 1973 (short stories).

Chapterhouse: Dune. New York: Putnam's, 1985.

Children of Dune. New York: Putnam's, 1976; Berkley, 1977.

Destination: Void. New York: Berkley, 1966. Revised 1978.

Direct Descent. New York: Ace Books, 1980 (novella).

The Dosadi Experiment. New York: Putnam's, 1977; Berkley, 1978.

The Dragon in the Sea. Garden City, N.Y.: Doubleday, 1956; New York: Ballantine, 1974 as *Under Pressure.*

Dune. Philadelphia: Chilton, 1965. New York: Berkley, 1977.

Dune Messiah. New York: Putnam's, 1969; Berkley, 1975.

Eye. New York: Berkley, 1985 (short stories).

The Eyes of Heisenberg. New York: Berkley, 1966.

God Emperor of Dune. New York: Putnam's, 1981; Berkley, 1982.

The Godmakers. New York: Putnam's, 1972; Berkley, 1973.

The Green Brain. New York: Ace Books, 1966.

The Heaven Makers. New York: Avon, 1968.

Hellstrom's Hive. Garden City, N.Y.: Doubleday, 1973 (Book Club Edition).

Heretics of Dune. New York: Putnam's, 1984; Berkley, 1985.

The Jesus Incident (with Bill Ransom). New York: Putnam's, 1979.

The Lazarus Effect (with Bill Ransom). New York: Putnam's, 1983.

Man of Two Worlds (with Brian Herbert). New York: Putnam's, 1986.

The Santaroga Barrier. New York: Berkley, 1968.

Soul Catcher. New York: Putnam's, 1972.

Whipping Star. New York: Putnam's, 1970; Berkley, 1970.

The White Plague. New York: Putnam's, 1982; Berkley, 1983.

The Worlds of Frank Herbert. New York: Ace Books, 1971 (short stories).

B. Nonfiction

1. Books

New World or No World. New York: Ace Books, 1970. A collection of articles prepared for the *Today* show during Earth Week 1970, edited and introduced by Herbert.

Threshold: The Blue Angels Experience. New York: Ballantine Books, 1973. Contains photos and screenplay from the documentary film.

Without Me You're Nothing (with Max Bernard). New York: Simon & Schuster, 1980. A guide to home computers and how to program them.

2. Essays
"Listening to the Left Hand." In *The Book of Frank Herbert.* New York: Daw Books, 1973, 205–218.
"Science Fiction and a World in Crisis." In *Science Fiction: Today and Tomorrow,* ed. Reginald Bretnor, 69–95. Baltimore: Penguin Books, 1975.

C. Unpublished and Miscellaneous Materials
The Special Collections Section of the Library at California State University, Fullerton, contains the Frank Herbert Archives. They maintain an inventory arrangement by opus number rather than a formal catalogue of their holdings. Descriptions such as working notes, working papers, typescript (which is the official manuscript modified by its condition), tape numbers, etc., used in my footnotes follow in general the descriptions chosen by the archives to graphically describe the actual holdings. In addition, Caedmon Records now has seven recordings available of Herbert reading selections from the *Dune* series, complete with Herbert's liner notes. *The Frank Herbert Soundbook* includes four cassettes and a program booklet. All selections are from the *Dune* trilogy (*Dune, Dune Messiah,* and *Children of Dune*), including Herbert's reading of the banquet scene discussed in chapter 2. See the catalogue published by *The American Audio Prose Library,* Fall 1986 through Summer 1987, for other titles.

SECONDARY SOURCES

Aldiss, Brian W. *Billion Year Spree: The True History of Science Fiction.* New York: Shocken Books, 1974. A literary history of science fiction which discusses Herbert's *Dune* and analyzes it briefly in relation to the norms of Campbellian science fiction.
Allen, L. David. *Frank Herbert.* Lincoln, Nebr.: Cliffs Notes, Inc., 1975. A monograph discussing Herbert's work, but focusing mainly on the unity and continuity of *Dune* and *Dune Messiah.*
Brigg, Peter. "Frank Herbert: On Getting Our Heads Together." In *Other Worlds: Fantasy and Science Fiction Since 1939,* ed. John Teunissen (Winnipeg: MOSAIC, 1980), 193–202. Examines Herbert's attitudes toward a collective mind versus the freedoms of the self. Finds "positive" collectivities in *Dune, The Green Brain,* and *The Santaroga Barrier* and a negative one in *Hellstrom's Hive.*
Grigsby, John L. "Asimov's 'Foundation' Trilogy and Herbert's 'Dune' Tril-

ogy: A Vision Reversed." *Science Fiction Studies* 8, no. 24 (July 1981):149–55. Examines similarities of movement and design in both series and concludes that the outcome of *Children of Dune* parodies and reverses the assumptions of Asimov.

Hand, Jack. "The Traditionalism of Women's Roles in Frank Herbert's *Dune*." *Extrapolation* 26, no. 1 (Spring 1985):24–28. Finds that all the important women of *Dune* act within the traditional areas of female activity in male-dominated societies. They express themselves as wives, mothers, sisters, and literary women, but always define themselves by male standards.

McNelly, Willis E. *The Dune Encyclopedia*. New York: Berkley, 1984. The single greatest source of information about the world Herbert created, cast in the form of an imaginary encyclopedia. An educated non-theologian's guide to the mysteries of Rakian religion.

———. "Frank Herbert." In *Science Fiction Writers,* ed. E. F. Bleiler, 337–85. New York: Scribner's, 1982. The best concise introduction to Herbert's intellectual themes.

Miller, David M. *Frank Herbert*. Starmont Reader's Guide No. 5. Mercer Island, Wash.: Starmont House, 1980. Finds a pattern of "dynamic homeostasis" in Herbert's fiction.

O'Reilly, Timothy. *Frank Herbert*. Recognitions Series. New York: Frederic Ungar, 1981. Argues that Herbert's *Dune* trilogy was set up to teach the reader a lesson in the dangers of hero worship. Good discussion of Herbert's other fiction.

Warrick, Patricia S. "The Open-System Model." In *The Cybernetic Imagination in Science Fiction*. Cambridge: MIT Press, 1980, 161–202. Argues that Herbert's *Destination: Void* is a unique literary accomplishment—a bildungsroman whose idea (the construction of an artificial consciousness) is the protagonist.

Index